DEPARTURE

DEPARTURE

Melodie M. Davis

HERALD PRESS
Scottdale, Pennsylvania
Waterloo, Ontario

Library of Congress Cataloging-in-Publication Data
Davis, Melodie M., 1951-
 Departure / Melodie M. Davis.
  p. cm.
 ISBN 0-8361-3549-0 (alk. paper)
 1. Davis, Melodie M., 1951- . 2. Mennonites—Biography.
3. American students—Spain—Barcelona—Biography.
BX8143.D38A3 1990
289.7′092—dc20
 [B]
             90-32027
             CIP

The paper used in this publication is recycled and meets the minimum requirements of American National Standard for Information Sciences—Permanence of Paper for Printed Library Materials, ANSI Z39.48-1984.

Contents

To Cathy, Deb, Nancy, and Tara

"People go abroad to admire the heights of mountains, the mighty billows of the sea, the long course of rivers, the vast compass of the ocean, and the circular motion of the stars, and yet pass themselves by."

—St. Augustine (paraphrased)

Author's Preface

By the end of my sophomore year in college, I was looking for a change. Without much long-range planning or preparation, I decided to investigate studying abroad.

I had *not* been majoring in language but was assured that the intermediate-level Spanish I had studied in college met the requirements of the Brethren Colleges Abroad study program. I was in for some surprises— and one of the best years of my life at the University of Barcelona, Spain.

But this is more than just a collection of adventures and learnings in a different culture. As a young adult, I was beginning to explore what I wanted to own or disown from my faith background, which was Anabaptist-Mennonite. I was longing for romance and a permanent relationship, yet realizing that I might remain single for a long time.

The events in this book are all true. My account is based on journal entries from that school year 1973-74, my complete letters home, and research into the period. Some names have been changed to protect privacy or to avoid confusion between several persons with the same name. In most cases I did not write down actual conversations word for word in my journal or letters. Thus the conversations included here reflect my best memory, which by now may be flawed. I do think they are true to character, although they may not have occurred precisely as they appear here.

Spain in 1973 was a very different county than it is today. Generalismo Francisco Franco, Spain's fascist dictator since 1939, was still alive and very much in charge. Sentiment against Franco was, by that time, intense and in some cases quite open, yet there was an undercurrent of secrecy and whispered rumors.

Catholicism was still the official state religion (until 1978). Protestants were few in number and not officially allowed to evangelize. For instance, they were not allowed burial in Catholic sections of cemeteries.

Franco died in 1975. By 1978, Spain had achieved a smooth transition to a democratic government with a new constitution. Today Barcelona is a flourishing mecca for many artists from all over Europe, a publishing center, and a popular tourist destination.

The book proceeds like life: I met people and had conversations that I hoped I would return to, but I never ran into those people again. By the end of the year, I was really only *beginning* to communicate well or understand some of my Spanish friends. A year's time is only an *orientation* to living abroad; now I understand mission board requirements for long-term service in other cultures.

I found no neat and tidy answers to questions about

myself, my future, or my faith. But I did receive threads, hints, and, at times, glorious confirmations that I was indeed where God wanted me for that year.

—Melodie M. Davis
Harrisonburg, Virginia

1

Locked In

"Oh, sex *before* marriage is much better," said my hostess, efficiently shaking out clean sheets for her postage stamp-sized spare bed. "It's more . . . spontaneous."

"But I don't believe in sex before marriage," I protested weakly in poor Spanish. "My friend and I, we just want to go *home*. We can't stay here."

"I'll make him a bed in the living room then," Mrs. Fernandez said, not really understanding why I'd pass up a chance to sleep with my friend.

"We need to leave *now*." I insisted again, growing more frantic. What would my roommates back at the boarding house think when they found out I hadn't come in all night?

"Please tell us how to get to the subway," I tried once more.

"The Metro is closed now. Too late. You have to stay here," said Mrs. Fernandez brokenly, for my benefit.

Anger edged my voice. "Well, what buses are running now?"

"The only one is far, far away. You'd have to walk too far. It's too hard to tell you how to get there."

She, I could tell, was beginning to get angry too. I was offending her.

I've heard of Spanish hospitality, I told myself, but this is ridiculous. There I was, virtually a prisoner in the apartment of a couple my friend and I had met only hours before, on an excursion to the amusement park at Mt. Tibidabo. The door was locked. It was one o'clock in the morning. How had I gotten myself into such a mess, anyway?

If my mother could see me now, I thought, as I had so often since leaving my quiet southern home.

The summer before departing for Spain, I spent working as a payroll clerk for the county school board in Blountstown, Florida, a typical, small, southern town. The best thing about my job was finding out what salaries all the county teachers and personnel made.

On my lunch hours, I prowled Main Street, hunting bargains for my trip and exercising for the same reason. At noon the town smelled of french fries as well as the earthy sweat of farmers who'd dashed to town to pick up a tractor part.

The Sam Ervin Watergate hearings were going all summer, but no one in that town was much interested. "If Nixon said he didn't know, he didn't know," one could hear at the drugstore coffee counter.

"Dadblamed communists. What's this country coming to anyway?"

There were three other people who worked in that office, people I said "Good morning" and "Good-bye"

11

to and that was about it. I never told them I was headed for Spain at summer's end for fear they'd think I thought I was better than they. Of all the sins to commit in a small southern town, getting uppity was the worst. Spain was a dark secret that got me through endless filing and typing, seeing only family, co-workers and church friends.

My first culture shock occurred not in Spain at all but enroute, in New York City. Our study group, organized through Brethren Colleges Abroad (BCA), was to meet for a day of orientation at the Tudor Hotel before flying to Spain. A former college roommate and I arranged to spend some time together that weekend. As we pushed our way through the crowds in Central Park on a Saturday afternoon, it struck me that I was seeing more people in a single afternoon than I had in my entire small-town summer. My head swam with all the languages and colors, and I felt like I was already abroad. With a male friend, we walked the streets of Greenwich Village at 1:00 a.m. and I pinched myself saying, "If Mom could see me now...."

It was different the next day though, as I set out by myself to find the hotel where the study group was gathering. I had explicit subway directions. Yet when I came out of Grand Central Station, looking at street signs to get my bearings, I must have looked every inch the Mennonite maiden I was. A huge man came up behind me and whispered, "Boo," and went hee-hawing down the street when my feet landed shakily back on the ground.

At last it was time to go to JFK Airport for a late-night chartered flight on an airline no one had ever heard of before. If I thought traveling abroad was going to be glamorous, I changed my mind as we waited through delays at a dirty, out-of-the-way terminal, dozing on the floor like homeless people. Small talk of name, state, and "where do you go to school" soon wore thin.

Bridgewater, University of Southern California, Drew, Goshen, Manchester, Millersville. So there was only one other person from a Mennonite school in the group and he was reading *Esquire* and chain-smoking.

"What's your major?"

Spanish. French. Language.

I appeared to be the only generalist, not yet having declared a major.

"Do you know Spanish very well?" I whispered this only if the other person looked as scared and uncertain as me. Two had lived in Argentina for a while. One was a native of Costa Rica. The guy from Goshen had spent a trimester in Central America.

If there had been a plane headed for home out of that miserable terminal, I might have taken it. Everyone else seemed to know at least one other person—or not care that they didn't. The girl from California looked so. . . . well, *like* a "California girl," with a lovely tan shown off by her halter dress. The guy from Goshen noticed too, of course. My own carefully chosen traveling-to-Europe suit with puffy sleeves and bow in back now seemed hopelessly high-schoolish.

A short, brown-haired girl dressed more like me flashed a wide smile. "I'm Cathy Bewley. Where are you from?"

"Blountstown, Florida. Or Eastern Mennonite Col-

lege in Virginia. But I grew up in Goshen, Indiana."
She grinned. I remembered seeing her parents with
her at the hotel, waving goodbye. "So where are you
from?"

"Elizabethtown—Church of the Brethren school."

I immediately relaxed. Brethren were "cousins" of
my denomination, Mennonite.

"You know, I'm surprised," I said. "For a Brethren
study program, there sure aren't many Church of the
Brethren kids."

"I know," Cathy confided. "Most Brethren colleges
don't have many Brethren kids."

At last the plane was loaded. There were hundreds
of other students like ourselves from *other* study programs, all destined for a year of study in Madrid, Se-
ville, or Granada. Our group was headed for Barcelona, in the northern region of Catalonia.

"Did you know they don't even talk Spanish very
much in Barcelona?" a girl named Lucille informed
me.

"Oh?" I tried to be noncommittal. My real knowledge of Spain was as inadequate as a sixth grader's social studies report lifted mostly from encyclopedias.

"They say that in homes and among friends, everyone really talks Catalan—a little like Spanish and
French."

"Oh, a dialect," I nodded.

"No, no, no, a language all it's own. Kind of like the
Provençal tongue of southern France," she said expertly.

Good grief. Here I didn't even know Spanish well,
and now I found out everyone talked another lan-

guage. Dear God, what had I gotten myself into? Would my "family" in Spain insist on talking Catalan? I started praying—for myself, my future, the captain of the airline no one had ever heard of.

The captain informed us we were approaching the coast of Spain. The land below was ribbons of brown and green, with low, distant mountains and a river here and there. I felt light years removed from my clerical summer, about to touch down on the greatest adventure of my twenty-one years.

The United States directors of BCA met us at the airport in Madrid and flew with us to Barcelona. Then a bus carried us to Lloret del Mar, a resort town along the Costa Brava, for five more days of orientation.

"Our hotel is right up there," said Professor Caman, pointing to a tiny sign at the top of a steep, narrow street. If I hadn't been so tired, I would have called it picturesque. No car could have made it through the street, and there was no porter nor a cart for our luggage.

"I can't go another step," one girl sputtered.

Professor Caman grinned maddeningly. "Now you know why the instructions said to travel light." Then he added, "Take your time; leave some of your luggage here. You can carry it up in shifts."

The fifty pounds of gear that had seemed so small in packing was now like Pilgrim's burden in Bunyan's *Pilgrim's Progress*. But then, with a sudden burst of pride or feminism or a runner's second wind, we gritted our teeth and got to the top without stopping.

A week of orientation next to the Mediterranean was idyllic, but I was anxious to meet my family. Getting out of a suitcase would be nice. Then after siesta one day, Caman called a conference.

"I'm sorry, but we haven't been able to find homes for all of you."

"What?"

"Yeah, five of you will have to go back to the U.S.," he deadpanned. "No, but I would like five female volunteers to live in a *residencia*, five who don't have their hearts set on living with a family."

"What's a residencia?" someone asked.

"Well, it's a residence, a little like a dorm but more like a boarding house. The family who runs it will give you breakfast and lunch everyday, but you'll be on your own for supper. BCA will give you back a portion of what you've paid, like an allowance, to buy your own supper each night. There will be other Spanish students and working women there too."

"We'll be on our own? No 'mother' to look after us? That doesn't sound so bad," said Tara of the striking halter top.

I supposed I should volunteer, since I knew a number of the students definitely preferred a family. I do too, I thought. Or would the freedom be nicer? It was the kind of choice where you didn't have much choice. I never liked to make waves or be a problem, so I volunteered for the residencia, feeling disappointed but noble.

One bright spot was that Cathy Bewley had volunteered too, along with Tara, a short, pretty girl named Deb, and a friendly girl named Nancy.

At the end of our week of orientation, Caman dropped us "women of the residencia" off on the pres-

16

tigious Avenida del Dr. Andreu, right at the base of Barcelona's Mt. Tibidabo.

"Barcelonians claim that Tibidabo is where the devil took Jesus for his third temptation," Caman quipped. "They say if the devil wanted Jesus to be tempted by the world's charms, the view from Tibidabo had to be the most tempting."

We smiled, never sure when to believe Caman.

"You can take the streetcar for just five *pesetas* and get a cog railroad to the top and read the legend for yourselves," he finished, waving in the direction of the mountain.

Caman introduced us to Señora Conchita at the residencia and gave us supper money for the first month. Suddenly we were really on our own.

It didn't take long to unpack fifty pounds of gear and get settled in our meager rooms. No posters, bedspreads, or normal college fare. Just plain, narrow bunk beds with thin mattresses, one drawer and one shelf each, and a small rod for hanging clothes (but no hangers).

Oh, well, all Barcelona was waiting to be explored, with a month of "supper money" smoldering in the pockets of our jeans. Where should we dine the first night?

"Let's just walk down the street and see what we find," Cathy suggested. It was already getting dark and we didn't know how to get anywhere else. So we walked a few blocks reading signs and hoping for a cheap place with plenty of atmosphere.

"Here it says chicken, forty-two pesetas."

"Hey, that's a pretty good price. About a dollar back home."

"I suppose they serve other things with it?"

"Sure."

"Well, why not?"

We entered what turned out to be a small, dark bar. The owner scrambled to find a table for five.

"Drinks?"

Did he mean cocktails or sodas, we asked each other in English. Tara was a little impatient. "The house wine," she said in fluent Spanish, being the one who had lived in Argentina for a year.

Well, was I going to drink wine this year or not? I knew already that water was often unavailable, and soft drinks usually cost twice as much as the house wine. What would Dad say?

Cathy was confidently asking for Coca-Cola. It figured. She was Church of the Brethren. Nancy went with wine. It didn't quite figure to me, for already she had made public her Christian witness. Deb and Tara professed nothing.

Outside, a waiter was wondering if my tongue would ever untie. Inside, a big ethical debate raged. To him, it was only a question of wine A or wine B. From my background, it was a question of heaven or hell.

I remembered a high school Bible teacher saying, "Jesus drank wine, but Jesus didn't drive." Well, I wouldn't be driving this year in the city either.

"The house wine," I mimicked, promising to explain myself to Cathy later.

"Well, so much for atmosphere," said Tara of our location at the rear of the less-than-spotless bar. Since it was a bar, the chicken was meant to be only a *tapa*, or appetizer, and nothing was served with it except ever-present Spanish bread.

"I can't believe we're paying forty-two pesetas for nothing but cold chicken," Deb grumbled.

"Bread's not bad though," Cathy said, grabbing another piece.

"I'll be so fat after a year on this bread," Deb groaned, nibbling a second piece, too. The service was slow, elegance was out of the question, and I imagined a year's suppers of nothing but garlicky chicken, fattening bread and cheap wine. I wondered what Mom and Dad were having for supper.

So this was Spain. A dirty bar. A lousy meal. A bare residencia that used to be a nun's convent. Five girls/women who had long since run out of small talk but were not yet real friends.

How would I survive the next nine months? There was no getting out of this. I had locked myself in.

2

Avenida del Dr. Andreu

I stood on the balcony off the upstairs bathroom at the residencia and shivered with expectancy—or maybe it was just the chill of the early September night. It was almost as though we were in the country, it smelled so full of vegetation and crickets and earth. I could hear dogs barking though and faintly, city traffic. This residencia would be coolly comfortable, if not homey. Besides, who wanted a Spanish "sister" to argue with anyway?

Still, an ache filled my throat as I went down the marble-looking steps to our first floor suite. I felt so alone. At the landing a stained glass window honored a Catholic saint, St. George somebody, and a dragon. I remembered that Caman had said something about nuns living in the basement.

Suddenly a *thing* moved on the window. A lizard. Horrors. A lizard in my new home. Then I smiled. The lizard looked a little like a dragon. Maybe St. George would help me slay some lizard-dragons this year.

On Saturday we did Barcelona like one-day tourists

instead of year-long ones. We snapped rolls of photos, not caring who heard us giggling like high schoolers, and flirted with Spanish boys.

Just a block from the residencia we could catch an underground train that hooked into the city's efficient and cheap subway system (Metro). We found our way to the city's center, a lovely square called Plaza Cataluña. At the center of the plaza was a huge multi-colored star laid into the concrete. We were soon to rely on that star as a marker for finding directions all over the city, and as a mistake-proof place to meet friends.

Directly off the plaza, streets spoked in every direction. None was more famous nor compelling than Las Ramblas, a wide boulevard of shops, cafes, flower stalls and book vendors beckoning for block after block. We found Barcelona's mini-Disneyland, Montjuich—and paid passing tribute to the statue of Christopher Columbus looking out to sea at the base of Las Ramblas. I saw enough city to tease me into feeling I'd just spent a day with a newfound love.

But by Sunday, a cold I'd been nursing for a week got the better of me. I decided to just unwind at the residencia.

"You'll never guess what we did!" Nancy exclaimed, coming in Sunday evening long after I'd donned my night gown. "We met the neatest Christian sailors, and they took us on their ship, and we had such pure fellowship," she bubbled on, her blue eyes dancing.

Jealously, I wondered how pure it was from the sailors' perspective. Then I felt ashamed of such thoughts.

"Well, tell me all about it," I said, smiling, glad for company after writing homesick-sounding letters all day.

"I wanted to call Mickey, you know, so I was down at the Centro Telefónico where Caman told us we could make long-distance calls easier.

"Well, the place was loaded with Navy guys, all trying to call home too, and I was helping them because none of them knew Spanish. Then I found out they were Christians, and they said they held a Bible study on board their ship. Of course, they were just really hungry to meet other Christians."

Nancy was truly beautiful when she was excited, so much so I couldn't even be envious. But *Navy* and *Christian* were such a contradiction in terms for me that I didn't know quite how to respond.

"That's neat, it really is," I said lamely.

"Oh, you poor dear with your awful cold," she sympathized. "Here I am going on and on about our wonderful day, and you were stuck in the room. How are you feeling, anyway?"

"Oh, I felt much better after I took that Contac. Cathy and I did go up Tibidabo this afternoon; the view's really as great as Caman claimed." After I told her more about Tibidabo, I encouraged Nancy to go on.

"Well, the sailors want us to come back and bring all our friends. You can imagine they're anxious for fellowship, stuck on board those ships with the same faces for months on end."

I wanted to ask how a Christian could serve in the Navy, but I already knew Nancy was dating a West

Point graduate, a man she called "the most beautiful Christian guy." As a female, I had always thought I didn't really need to face the military issue.

I had been on old ships before, but never on a real, active United States Navy ship. Now that the U.S. no longer had troops involved in Vietnam, a number of ships patrolled the potentially volatile Mediterranean. Frequently the ships docked in Barcelona for R and R.

It sounded like fun to go on board a *real* ship and, to a Mennonite, nothing short of going into the camp of the enemy.

Growing up, I had been taught that it was wrong to kill. Period. A Christian could have no part in violence. Belonging to any branch of the military in any way was to join yourself with "the killing machinery," impossible for the Christian. There is no such thing as a just war.

Furthermore, I was raised on CO tales from World War II. CO stands, of course, for conscientious objector, *not* commanding officer like the women who worked in an office with my mother used to think.

Mom was a secretary during the war. Her boyfriend, who later became my father, was away—like all the men. Mom would tell her colleagues her boyfriend was a CO. When they mistakenly assumed commanding officer, I'm told my mom didn't always bother to correct them.

Daddy's "war" stories concerned the misadventures of mentally ill patients at a hospital where he worked, getting locked in the morgue there and yelling "Hey, I'm not dead" till someone got him out. Pretty mild stuff as war stories go, but it was the lore I was raised on.

Our heroes were, instead, the Anabaptist ancestors who really had died for their beliefs. On our bookshelf at home sat a huge book we dragged out only when a two-year-old needed to be boosted at the dining table or when we wanted to be horrified senseless. It was the *Martyrs Mirror*, with page upon page of Christians who had been tortured for their faith.

Somehow it was instilled in me that the only cause worth dying for was the cause of Christ, not one's country. And no cause justified killing—or even resorting to violence or civil disobedience.

Like my mother in her office, I found I didn't want to make waves. "Oh, that would be neat," I told Nancy, when she invited me to join the Bible study on the ship the next Friday night.

But first came Monday, the Monday of a new school year in a wonderful new city. We were excited about riding the Metro to class. Someone told us about buying month-long passes to save money and time waiting in lines. By the end of the week, we learned to go to the front of the train while it was still traveling to save steps in the station when getting off. We caught on to using the right exit from the underground station so we didn't have to cross the street in crazy traffic at the university's door.

I knew enough not to expect a quiet, tree-lined campus like we were used to at home. But I wasn't expecting just a large cement building in the heart of downtown Barcelona. This was the old campus. I learned that the new part of the university, on the outskirts of Barcelona, was a little more "campusy."

Once inside the cement building, though, a quiet

courtyard with a fountain and little benches greeted students. Off the courtyard were doors to classrooms on two levels. A third basement level housed a student cafe and maintenance quarters.

Through another gateway, one found another courtyard with a similar arrangement of classrooms organized around a quadrangle on two levels. Faculty and administrative offices were tucked in a maze I never did figure out. And beyond one of the courtyards was an actual garden, with benches and quiet places for studying or intimate conversation.

We took the Metro all the way back to our residencia on Avenida del Dr. Andreu after morning classes (a good twenty-minute commute). *Comida*, the main meal of the day, was served beginning around 1:00 in the afternoon. This was early by Spanish standards, but nothing short of torture for our stomachs, which were still on U.S. time clocks.

The *pan* (bread) would arrive first, in the little dumbwaiter that brought us our meals. We gobbled the bread while waiting for the first course of soup or runny mashed potatoes. The second course, usually meat, came by itself on a plate. Then came dessert, usually one piece of fresh fruit, also served alone. The Spanish girls usually ate their fruit with a knife and fork.

On such a diet we would have lost weight, but my downfall was the dollar of "supper" money we were allowed every day. We scrounged to make that dollar go as far as possible but ate well for our evening meal, which we usually fixed in our rooms on a makeshift, single-burner camping stove. We feasted on soup, omelets, bread, cheese, yogurt, fruit, more bread, and plenty of cookies dunked in *café con leche* (coffee with milk).

By the end of our first week of real classes, the routines were already becoming old. "I've eaten more bread this week than in my whole life," Deb grumbled, playfully pinching her tiny new paunch.

"I'm already tired of the Metro," groaned Tara. "The stench is horrible down there."

"Can you believe how tight everyone wears their clothes?" Cathy added. "What I wouldn't do to see a guy in pants that actually fit!"

"Wouldn't it be great to see a real chef's salad for lunch?" I chimed in, "instead of one little pathetic tomato for garnish?"

"Or how about a Big Mac?" Deb added, and we all clenched our pillows in agony.

"Sh, maybe Conchita will hear us downstairs," worried Nancy.

With our homesickness, joining a bunch of sailors on their ship didn't sound like a bad way to spend our second Friday night in Barcelona. Cathy, Nancy, and I went from the residencia. We were joined by Bonnie, who lived with a Spanish family.

We were already pegged as different from the group, being "Christians." The pigeonhole made me uneasy. Yes, I was a Christian, but I didn't want other BCA kids to think I thought I was better than they. I knew there were other kids in the group who *did* consider themselves Christians but weren't about to have *anything* to do with U.S. sailors in port.

We walked up a wide gangplank, just like in the movies. Someone gave us the okay to go on board.

"Just like that?" Cathy wanted to know. I gave her a grin. Was she like me, feeling a little ambivalent?

A sailor led us through skinny halls and funny oval doors, until we came to a large room with a bunch of guys sprawled on the floor. They all looked so young and like they had just stepped off the streets of Blountstown instead of Barcelona.

They were talking about how the war in Vietnam *could* have been won if only the U.S. had used more force. Now even the office of the presidency was being laughed at around the world. It was a hard time to be a U.S. sailor in a foreign port, one said.

As the formal sharing time got underway, they talked about being laughed at because they were Christian, their struggles with tobacco and alcohol, and being away from a young wife and child. We heard about loneliness and boredom and feeling different because a weekend of R and R didn't mean quite the same thing for these guys as for their shipmates.

We heard new Christians fearing that, if they weren't careful, they would soon backslide. We heard rejoicing over a reported revival at West Point Academy back in the States. The story there was that one chaplain had retired (or been fired?) from his job for giving too many successful altar calls. (Maybe it was still dangerous to be a Christian in the U.S. after all.)

For the first time I realized what a desolate place those ships would be if indeed there were *no* Christians in the Navy who could be "salt" in a difficult place. Did God allow different Christians to stress different truths as part of a divine plan?

Yet how could I depart even this far from the truths I was raised on? Would *I* lose my saltiness?

27

3

Olé Flamenco!

Tara removed a cigarette from a pack of one of Spain's cheaper brands, as we all sat around the table in her room after supper.

"Isn't it rotten that the government chose this year to change Spain's universities over to a semester system?" she groaned.

"Yeah, I heard Jim's thinking about going home," Nancy remarked. "What if our colleges don't accept these credits Caman is scurrying to arrange?"

"They'd better," said Deb. "I didn't pay $2,800 for *nothing*, I hope."

The plan, as Caman had outlined to us in the university patio that morning, was for him to hire several Spanish profs to teach us for about eight weeks, until Christmas vacation. Then we'd enroll in regular university classes in mid-January.

The good news was that, in addition to the planned group trip to Madrid at the end of the first six-week term, we would have an extra week of vacation to do anything we liked.

"When did you start smoking?" Deb asked Tara.

"Well, I figure to make friends, to look Spanish, I better do as they do," Tara replied.

"I can't believe how many girls smoke!" Deb exclaimed. "I mean, I don't have anything against it, but *everyone* smokes!"

Tara tapped an ash and took another drag with the smoothness of a hooker. "These are pretty awful," she admitted coolly. "But I certainly can't afford imported U.S. cigarettes here."

"Why, what do they cost?" I ventured. This was one way I could safely enter the conversation.

"Paul's buying Marlboros, and they're nearly a dollar. About double what they are back home," Tara said, puffing. "You can get some cigarettes here for as little as *un duro.*" A duro was worth about ten cents at the time.

Well, I told myself, as I withdrew to my room, I may try an occasional glass of wine this year, but I certainly won't smoke just to "be like the Spaniards."

I definitely needed to study. Our first test was coming up. It felt awful to be considered the dumbest, or perhaps next-to-dumbest, in the class for the first time in my life. What if I really flunked?

I felt high two days later when I learned I not only passed but with high grades.

The trip by bus took us through vintage Spain. Starting from the coastal lands near Barcelona, we passed through miles of foothills before nearing the small mountains of central Spain. The sun, unmerciful even in early October, was baking the countryside to dust.

I spied my first checkerboard vineyards. We were close enough to the rows that I could almost smell the luscious grapes ripening. The bus passed a bereted man. His donkey was pulling a cart laden with grapes —picture perfect. Here and there were isolated houses, whitewashed and bare, but brightened by orange, tiled roofs and geraniums—always geraniums—beneath the windows.

I looked at the mountains in the distance and wondered what tales they hid of the centuries of soldiers who had marched over them. The effects of years of occupation were well-documented: fatalism about life, (what will be will be), a distrust of outsiders, camaraderie with one's own kind, and a fierce regionalism that survived when one's national identity changed at the whim of distant kings.

In the villages, small clusters of men leaned on canes; their cheeks were like withered apples. So many old women wore black dresses, because black was a widow's color for the rest of her life, not just for a year.

Although it shouldn't have, one thing surprised me, ruining the pictures I was taking in my mind. Telephone and electric lines threaded through every scene. End of fantasy.

A new city to explore! So what do U.S. girls do? Go shopping! We found a Spanish version of K Mart and oohed over bargains. Then we gladly curled up in our three-star hotel at the end of an exhausting first day.

"Find any bargains?" Tara asked, like she was really interested.

"I'd like to find a leather coat over here, but I was

mostly just looking so far." I was glad to find something I could actually talk about with Tara.

"Yeah, what's the rush? We've got a whole year," she laughed and for a minute she was just another college girl. "I want to find a good buy on a guitar soon, though. I'm hoping to start taking classical guitar lessons when the new term starts."

"Oh, that would be fun. Cathy's looking for one too, you know." That was dumb. Of course she knew. They were roommates back at the residencia.

"Well, I'm turning in early," Tara said, grabbing her makeup bag and heading for the bathroom.

"Yeah, sounds like a full day tomorrow."

"Boy, this *is* luxury for Spain," Tara said, pausing as she brushed her teeth. "When Pete and I went to Andorra with the Camans, we had to use a communal bathroom out in the hall."

She said it so casually. Of course, that hadn't meant she and Pete slept together, did it? Pete's early interest in Tara had been disappointing, since he easily took my vote for best-looking guy in the group.

I feigned sleep by the time Tara had finished in the bathroom.

The next morning our group traveled out to the Valley of the Fallen, a memorial to all who died in Spain's bloody civil war. It was also the future burial place of Generalisimo Franco—as if he wanted to insure ahead of time that Spain would honor him with a memorial. A tomb on layaway!

On the way back to our hotel, Paco, the Spanish professor who was our group's coleader, looked as though he was about to present us with a gift. "Tonight," he said, as his black eyes danced, "we go *tasca* hopping."

Of course, he couldn't speak a word of English, at least none that he would share with us. Because Paco was from the southern most region of Spain, Andalusia, we had as hard a time understanding Paco as a New Yorker hearing a Georgian. He clipped the ends of sentences and rat-a-ta-tated his words when he momentarily forgot he was speaking to slow learners.

"Melodia," he said, smiling at me. "Have you ever eaten *calamares*"?

I froze, then stuttered, "Calamares?"

I had bumbled around trying to talk Spanish to him so often it was almost a joke. I knew he dismissed me as hopeless, the dumbest in the class. It was not a pretty thought. At the bottom of my class for the first time in my life.

He threw back his head laughing, having gotten the response he expected. Then, more kindly, he said, "Someone tell Melodia what calamares are."

Fried squid. Squishy, smelly tentacles that people actually ate. But deep fried so they tasted a little like fried onion rings.

Well, it would take more than a little breading and french-fry grease to get me to put anything with little suction cups in my mouth.

Paco had good intentions, even if his forthrightness —apparently another Andalusian trait—sometimes left me embarrassed. Ever the professor, he was not just making fun of me for not knowing what calamares were but really trying to teach me something. Always trying to draw me out. What he didn't know was that even the best of my friends back home had trouble doing that.

"And then, after the tapas, we will have flamenco!" Paco proclaimed. "Good, pure flamenco—not the stuff for the tourists."

It was 8:30 p.m. when those of us going tasca hopping gathered in the hotel lobby, the customary hour for going out for a Spanish evening on the town. But I was already tired from a long day of touring. Tasca hopping is kind of like grazing from one tray of delectable hors d'oeuvres to the next. Only in this case, you graze from one bar to the next for that bar's specialty. Paco knew the best places, and we gathered around him like sponges.

By the time we got to the bar featuring the fried squid, I was feeling lighthearted. Paco was skillful enough at applying peer pressure that I mustered up enough courage for one bite. It squished inside, but not bad. In fact, a little like good fried chicken. We tried fried mushrooms and shrimp and variations of omelets, until finally Paco allowed us to order a dessert cake to top off our progressive supper.

This was all appetizer, though, to the main course of the evening, a flamenco show performed by real Andalusian flamenco artists. A guitarist crooned haunting love ballads that went on forever. Lone dancers interpreted the song by tapping, shimmering, and gyrating with unbelievable control. It was a dance that called up the very soul of Spain.

"Bueno! Vale! Flamenco puro!" (Great! It's worth it! Genuine flamenco) called Paco and a number of fans around us at poignant points in the performance. It was not considered rude to interrupt, but a compliment. Appreciation for a performance rightly ex-

33

plodes. It doesn't need to wait for the proper moment, Paco explained.

After the show we headed back to the hotel. My head was swimming. So much beauty, so much art, so much history, so much experience—all in one day.

My heart's so full. You are so good, God. You created so much, I praised in my soul as we walked. It was close to 2:00 a.m., but one hardly thought of being scared on Spain's streets even at that hour. A semi-police state in the form of protection by Franco's Guardia Civil (civil police) had it's good points.

It did not surprise me that Tara was not in our room. I was glad to be alone. No worry about saying the right thing.

But why did it shock me when I happened to notice a suspicious little case of pills in Tara's makeup bag on the bathroom shelf? Why had she left her bag open? I chided her, then myself, feeling like a sneak. She'd probably just been in a hurry when getting ready to go out.

I immediately recognized the case as containing the same brand of birth control pills my married sister took.

So Tara probably *had* slept with Pete. And again I felt like a little girl.

4

Three Girls in Paris

In the morning, there was all of the Prado to make me forget my confusion of the night before. The Prado is Spain's greatest museum, arguably one of the greatest collections of art in the world. I knew enough about the frustration of trying to see art museums with a group of others that I discreetly slipped off alone to meet and meditate on the masters, one by one. First the Spanish artists—Velásquez, Goya, El Greco, Picasso. Then others—Raphael, Titian, Brueghel, Rubens. They all gave me goose bumps.

"What was your favorite?" Nancy asked over supper.

"I suppose it was Goya's *Family of Carlos IV*," I said, "with Goya coyly painting himself into the background."

"Wasn't it neat how the Grecos looked so much more elongated in real life, standing there looking up at them," commented Deb. It felt so sophisticated to be discussing art like professors or something.

"Just wait till we get to the Louvre," Nancy smiled.

She was dreaming of the following week, when Nan, Deb, and I would be in Paris.

"I think I finally understand Professor Beldor and his love for his art slides," I laughed. "We always thought he was coming from another planet when he'd go into ecstasy talking about this or that piece of art he'd seen." The other girls laughed too. Apparently there was a Professor Beldor at every college.

If the Prado was a fully satisfying entree, a side trip to the ancient city of Toledo was the dessert to our week near Madrid. We climbed to the bluff overlooking the Tagus River and looked down from the view El Greco had painted into his famous *View of Toledo.*

It was as if time had frozen. Life in Toledo was still cobbled streets and children playing in uniforms and long-robed bishops hurrying down tight alleyways. It was, again, the black-garbed widow, bereted men, and a damascene artist hammering gold on the little turtles, jewelry, and swords sold in the tourist shops.

But most of all, it was Toledo's cathedral, where the plain chant of the priest was positively medieval, haunting, and powerful enough to produce shivers. Sun streamed through the high rose window. It was everything a Gothic cathedral should be, invoking a sense of the eternal most high God, solemnity, awe.

It was a time of worship that stirred my soul. Yet I wondered, like a heathen, how Catholics could stand so much ritual and routine. All that crossing themselves and kneeling and highbrow Latin.

Back outside, the brilliant sun made me blink.

Three days and two bus trips later, Nancy, Deb, and I found ourselves in front of another cathedral, the

Notre Dame in Paris, France. The trip from Barcelona took seventeen hours, including three hours worth of bus stops.

Originally, I had planned to go to Paris alone, to look for a couple who had visited our home many years before. But Nancy and Deb also had Paris on their "must see" list, and so it was that we three landed on the streets of Paris with only a map and no idea where to begin. Thanks to *Europe on $5 a Day* (by Arthur Frommer) and information from Caman, we did know we wanted a cheap hotel in the Saint Michel area.

With our suitcases and maps, we must have looked as disoriented as we felt, because three people soon asked if we needed help. One explained Paris' fantastic Metro system. Another told us where cheap hotels were but said there was some kind of convention in Paris that weekend so "good luck finding a hotel." Who says Parisians are cold toward U.S. citizens?

But if they are, the next guy from the U.S. we ran into gave us a hint as to why. He had been wandering around the city for three days already and could only tell us the general direction of the Sorbonne. We were standing practically in front of Notre Dame, but he didn't know what it was or where the Louvre was.

We dragged our luggage along St. Michel Boulevard to the area of the Pantheon. We forked over one half franc (then about 13 cents) each to use a public john, (and were astounded that men were in the same room hidden only by a panel). Then we found a room in the Hotel des Grands Hommes, right on the square of the Pantheon.

"Frommer says this hotel has sadly declined in recent years and is only for 'hardy' young tourists," I said, reading from our *Europe on $5 a Day* bible.

We creaked up bare, dirty steps to the third floor and opened a door. A lone bulb hung from the center of the room. The beds looked lumpy. (Had the linens even been changed?) A hastily constructed partition masqueraded as a bathroom. It held only a sink and a bidet. No toilet or, needless to say, bath. Holes gaped through the flooring.

"Where's the bathroom in this place?" wondered Deb, and went out into the hall. She found a little sign. "I think it says the bathroom is on the next floor. Great." Of the three of us, she was the only one who knew any French at all.

The toilet was worse than an outdoor john, but at least it wasn't one of the stand-up versions frequent in Paris. "Probably rats in here," shivered Nancy.

"Well, the price is right," I said, not enthusiastic but trying to be hopeful. "Thirteen francs a person, including breakfast, remember."

"At least there's hot water and heat," Deb chimed in.

"We won't be spending much time in the room anyway," agreed Nan.

"Outside, it's Paris!" finished Deb. "Our mothers will never have to know." We all laughed and hurried to wash up.

For the next seven hours we hit the streets, discovering Paris' famous high prices but also a moderately priced department store that seemed to be full of Parisians rather than tourists. In many ways we were an unlikely trio to spend a week in Paris together. Nancy was so devout, quick to say "praise the Lord," but wisely watching herself around Deb.

"It's not that I don't believe in God," Deb said as we warmed ourselves over café au lait and pastries that cost too much. "I just don't see how any one can know for *sure*. That's why I'm an agnostic."

How could any one so nice, so normal, call herself agnostic? The very word seemed to doom her. How could anyone so nice and normal be doomed? "*I* don't see how any one could see all we've seen and *not* know there's a God," Nan replied, her perfect face as earnest as a five-year-old's.

"I never found any meaning in the Catholic church I grew up in," Deb went on. "And even now, all the Christians I see are so inconsistent. For instance, how come you and Nan will drink wine, but Cathy won't?"

So it was true. Non-Christians really did watch the behavior of Christians, trying to make it stack up. I always suspected that was just something Sunday school teachers used to tell us to get us to behave.

"Well, I never drank wine before," I stumbled while Deb waited. "But I've decided that this year, in Europe, with wine being cheaper than soft drinks and more available than good water—well, it just seems less hassle," I finished in my usual wishy-washy way.

"And my parents always drank," Nancy threw in. "Dad would come home from work, and Mom would fix cocktails. Sometimes they'd let me have a sip."

I was quiet. How could Nancy grow up drinking cocktails, be considering marriage to someone who was an officer-in-training at West Point Academy, and call herself Christian?

For tonight, though, our differences paled in comparison to seeing if we could survive a night in what we'd have called a flophouse in the States. I was so glad I wasn't alone like I had planned. If the hotel was miserable, at least I had company.

On Sunday morning we slept late, but Nan finally pulled back what was left of the muslin rag at the window.

"Cloudy." Nan laid back in bed. "Oh, well. What do you say we get over to Notre Dame in time for mass?"

"Sure," Deb grinned. "My mother would be proud. I haven't been to mass in a long time."

The hotel dining room was so ramshackle it was almost homey. Two croissants for breakfast, butter, jam and plenty of tea or coffee, all on the house. We got to Notre Dame just in time for the 11:30 a.m. mass. Just hearing the pipe organ was worth the seventeen-hour bus trip. But the actual mass in French was a little too much. We were glad when it was over.

We went up to explore the famed gargoyles along the roof. From the roof, we could see the Eiffel Tower against the cold gray sky. The murky Seine meandered beneath her oft-painted bridges. And the little art sellers and their displays of prints, originals, and junk attracted Sunday strollers on their way to the Louvre.

Sunday was free day at the museum, and so it seemed that all of Paris, half of the U.S., and generous sprinklings of people from the rest of the world were there. But in an afternoon's time, we could pay only passing respect to all the greats. How pitiful it seemed to hurry past world-renowned masterpieces, simply because a bathroom called more strongly.

5

The Pits

It was good to be "home." After taking only partial baths from a bidet and washbowl for six days, the shower at the residencia felt wonderful—even though the hot water from the little gas-powered heater always gave out in just minutes.

Seeing all the other kids was like a mini-homecoming too, all of us fresh with "can you top this" travel stories. We wondered aloud whether what we were reading in *La Vanguardia*, Barcelona's main paper, was true. It reported that support for President Nixon had weakened dramatically since Nixon fired Watergate special prosecutor Archibald Cox.

"Caman says the Spanish papers exaggerate all the time. They just plain make up the stuff," said Deb.

"It can't really be that bad," Linda laughed.

Just then Caman walked into the patio. "I've got some good news and some bad news."

"We get another week off from school?" quipped Paul, a huge guy better known as "Buddha."

"I don't think your colleges back home would go for

41

that. But, as you've probably heard, Madrid has decided not to open the university at all until January."

Most of us hadn't been exactly spending our vacations keeping up on the dreary internal affairs of Spain. But the more politically aware complained, "You told us we couldn't believe everything we read in the *Vanguardia*."

Caman smirked. "So what's new about that? I hope you don't believe everything back home, either!"

"Okay, okay, so what's going on?" asked Deb.

"Well, somehow it's related to the student strikes and the delay in opening this fall. The University of Barcelona has been the center of student protests ever since the first ones erupted back in '68.

"Political leaders here want more control in general. Now students can't get a whole term's work done anyway. Plus, they're wanting to switch over to a semester system. That's the simplest I can explain it."

"I can't imagine a country just being able to close all the universities!" commented Pete.

"Remember, this isn't a democracy," countered Caman. "The government does what it wants."

"What's the *good* news?" Tara asked.

"Well, first, you can be glad you're not Spanish students," Caman went on, anxious for the lesson in practical politics to fully sink in.

"They're stuck. But I've got everything worked out for you. I've lined up some of the best Spanish profs to give our group private classes in literature, anthropology, history, and art. In some ways, this will be better. You won't yet be immersed into classes with Spanish students. These profs will be able to take their time and answer your questions.

"Once you get into the regular university classes, you'll hardly know the teachers. They come to class a half hour late or not at all, lecture for an hour from notes they could have handed out on paper, then leave," Caman finished.

"So when do we start?"

"This evening, after siesta. Here's the schedule," Caman said as we whipped out our notebooks.

Several of us gathered later in the university café. "I'm definitely thinking about going home," said Jim. "I just don't think I'm getting a good education this year."

"I wonder how much of my money I could get back," wondered Nancy, who had more than her education to think about. One of her boyfriends had wired her a dozen long-stemmed roses on our return from France.

The cups of hot coffee with milk felt good in our hands, surrounded as we were by the chilly, stone walls of the university compounds. I wondered if my school back home would accept all these unusual credits.

"I'm going to enroll in that German class in the language institute now," Cathy said.

"And I'm glad I have my French and classical guitar lessons," Tara added.

Unfortunately, we didn't all have money to spend on private classes. "What I hate is that this means there won't be many Spanish women moving into the residencia as promised," I said. "I'm never going to *have* to practice my Spanish."

"Speaking of the residencia," said Cathy, "let's go

there. I'm freezing. Who ever thought Spain would get so cold so quickly?"

But the residencia held little comfort. It seemed there was an unwritten law in Spain, or an actual policy in most apartment leases, that no heat was turned on in buildings until November 1. I put my housecoat over the top of my street clothes and piled a blanket over that to rest for siesta that day, not sure if my spirits or my toes were colder.

In about two months it would be Christmas. If I could only make it until Christmas, I could surely make it through the year. Maybe Mom and Dad would visit at Christmas. We had been writing letters about the possibility.

How little I knew about Spain before I came! Even now I was tempted to rest on my small pile of learnings, like an instant expert.

Nancy, Cathy, Deb, and Tara. Could it be only two months that I had known them? At least we'd gone beyond name, major, and hometown conversations. Nancy was such a dear, but still I felt dowdy and unattractive around her.

And then there were our differences on matters of faith. Nancy was trying to get us to use the Spanish version of the "Four Spiritual Laws" with students we met. Cathy felt, like me, that the gospel couldn't be reduced to four short laws. But we both felt guilty and unchristian when we did not appear enthusiastic. I also hesitated to get involved because I knew this would only push Deb farther away from Christianity.

Christians often worry about how to be salt in a non-Christian environment and how to avoid "all appearance of evil," like Grandma preached. Maybe it was just as important to worry about not *rubbing* salt into the wounds of someone who has had a bad experience in the church, and to avoid all appearance of being "better than thou."

And Tara. While her California coolness no longer scared me, she didn't hide her "sleepovers" with a Spanish guy she had just met. Would I ever feel the same kinship with these girls I had come to feel with Ruthi and Jan and Mim in our community house the year before?

We met our new interim profs that evening. Jesús was a young, hazel-eyed Spanish man with crazy hair and an engaging smile. He was to teach anthropology, but he could have been teaching us our ABCs and I would have been just as impressed.

Then there was Dr. Arbonna. He was a fatherly grammar teacher who had already been teaching us the past six weeks during our orientation time. He was to school us further in contemporary Spanish idioms.

Our other two profs were Paco, teaching history, and his fiancée, Maria Angeles, teaching art history. Both had also taught us during the orientation period, and, of course, Paco was coleader of the group.

Maria Angeles had to take the prize for enunciating Spanish the slowest and clearest. I could write down almost every word she said. I could also understand most of what the professors said, because many words had the same Latin bases as our English or somehow sounded like an English equivalent.

Paco was the exception. He continued to fire at us like a machine gun, but that was how most people on the street sounded anyway, if we could understand them at all. Catalan was definitely the idiom of choice in this separatist area of Spain. It was a tongue learned at home and used to show that you were pro-Catalan.

Soon it was November 1, "All Saint's Day." There were no classes; all shops were closed. It was more than just a Catholic holdover from the Middle Ages. People used it as a Memorial Day to visit the graves of loved ones, as well as a day to honor all the traditional saints of the church.

People officially got out their winter clothes for the first time that day. Conchita, at the residencia, had purchased exquisite little pastries for dessert at our midday meal (holidays being the only time we had any sweets served at the residencia). But the best event of the day? Conchita turned on the heat!

"I can't believe what a difference this heat makes in my attitude," smiled Deb. "When we were cold, I just couldn't make myself do anything. I couldn't concentrate on my studies. I just wanted to eat to get warm. I've even been thinking about taking up smoking to keep my hands warm and to keep from eating."

I laughed. A smoking roommate. Somehow the idea wasn't as abhorrent as it would have been only two months ago. I had smoke in my face all day anyway.

That evening several of us had been invited to supper by a couple from the U.S. that we had met at a church, the Iglesia Biblica Ebenezer. On the way back to the residencia after the meal, we ran into one of the Spanish girls from the residencia on the subway.

"*Ola*, Melodia and Cathy," Maria said, and I was a little surprised that she even knew our names. She always seemed so distant and reserved, as though she thought she was better than us.

"*Dónde trabajas?*" we asked to find out where she worked. She spoke slowly and carefully about her job in a downtown office. She, of course, had had the day off too. She asked how we had enjoyed our holiday.

We explained that we had just had an "American" supper. She wanted to know how it was different from a Spanish supper. Maybe there was hope for making friends with the Spanish women in the residencia after all.

The next day the mail brought a letter from Mom and Dad. It said that soybean prices were extra high this year, and they would definitely meet me in Europe the day after Christmas. They could spend about two weeks with me, until the projected opening of the university in mid-January. I was ecstatic!

Their love—shown by this new sacrifice—poured over the ocean to me. It filled up the empty spaces in my longings. It chased away the aloneness except for what I felt in two places: the deep place inside where a young woman desires love different from what parents can give. And the place in my head where I still worried that I would never be as beautiful or as kind as Nancy.

6

Out on the Street

"Que gracia!" said a young man as I passed a construction site on the street.

I hid a smile and kept on walking. Whenever my self-esteem was at low ebb, Spanish men made me feel beautiful. In the U.S., the catcall of a construction worker might have been cause for contempt. But how can you get mad at a statement that translates something like "what loveliness!"

"In Spain we call the compliments that men pass out on the street *piropos*," lectured Dr. Arbonna in his colloquial Spanish class one day. " 'Piropo' literally means 'bouquet,' and that is what most are meant to be —a bouquet tossed to you with no intentions beyond that. Many are improvised poetry, lovely and imaginative. For example, many use comparisons or similes: 'Your eyes are like the stars at night.' Some are vulgar, but not always."

Tara raised her hand. "Well, why don't professional businessmen or even most of the guys at the university give out these piropos if they're so poetic?" We chuckled.

"Good point," agreed Dr. Arbonna. "In some ways, it's a custom from our past. Then Spanish young men and women weren't allowed to mix and most of the courting had to be done on the street, under the watchful eye of grandmother sitting on a balcony." Arbonna paced the front of the classroom.

"So if a young man saw a girl he liked, he thought up a beautiful poem that described her graces and tossed it to her while she passed by with her mother or friends. Today, with social customs more open and with much more sexual freedom, the piropo is not so needed, especially among the educated."

"I still feel like I'm in a meat market," retorted Deb. "How are we supposed to respond?"

"Like the Spanish women. If it's a nice compliment, a shy smile is okay, and keep on walking. If it's vulgar, pretend you didn't even hear it. If you let yourselves get picked up on the street, it reinforces their stereotype that U.S. women are 'easy,' " Arbonna finished in fatherly fashion.

Walking the streets was one of my favorite pastimes —not to pick up piropos *or* men but to explore new parts of Barcelona. After the newness of being a stranger in a strange land had worn off, I needed to continually find ways to keep fresh, to keep learning new things.

From the beginning of the year, we searched for a church home. We started first with an Anglican congregation made up of English-speaking people from a number of different countries. It was just a couple blocks from the residencia. The people had been wonderfully friendly. On our first day they invited us to stay for lunch, conversation, and also afternoon tea in the English tradition.

It had been almost too good. While we felt immediately at home, we knew that what we really wanted to do this year was involve ourselves in a Spanish-speaking congregation.

Our next find was the Iglesia Biblica Ebenezer, a store-front-type church led by a U.S. pastor-missionary couple. They sang a lot of U.S.-style choruses there (in Spanish). While it was small and friendly, we really wanted to find a Protestant Spanish church led and pastored by Spaniards.

So we were delighted to find the Iglesia Evangelica Bautista de Gracia (Evangelical Grace Baptist Church), with about 400 attenders. We usually referred to it simply by the name of the street, Calle Verdi. It offered the advantages of a much larger congregation, like a large youth group, a choir, lots of programs.

An additional bonus was Spanish pastor Jose M. Martinez, who enunciated his Spanish with all the slowness and clarity of our professor Maria Angeles! For the first time, I could actually understand a Spanish sermon. Alas, most of the people, including the pastor, were native Catalans. So among themselves they naturally spoke Catalan, even though the worship services were in Castellaño (Castilian—Spanish as it is spoken in Spain).

"You don't have to talk 'Castellaño' for us," we protested to the youth, over and over, as they rattled to each other in the more comfortable Catalan and then stopped themselves because of us.

"Oh no, that would be rude. You're only here for a short while. We will talk Castellaño."

Many of them were also studying English. Some, the pastor's son Pedro among them, spoke it like natives. But they were good about making us practice our Spanish.

"You are in Spain. You talk Spanish," scolded one friend named Lydia. "When I come to the U.S., then we will talk English."

It was easy to find English-speaking people wherever we went. One Saturday morning I got up the nerve to open a conversation with Vicky, a Bolivian young woman who lived upstairs at the residencia. Vicky not only knew English as well as we did, she was proud of speaking it with a U.S. accent, rather than with the formal English accent usually taught in Spain. She always insisted on talking to us in English. I was never sure if that was to show us how much she knew or because she couldn't bear our murdering of the Spanish tongue.

"So what do you study, Vicky?" I said casually on my way through the study room after breakfast.

"Business administration and economics," she said, looking as though she didn't mind the interruption.

"Ugh, I always thought that sounded boring."

"Oh, it really isn't, not at all. A business degree is just a passport to so many jobs, especially in Bolivia."

"So do you plan to return to Bolivia?"

Vicky nodded, her auburn hair teased in a carefree style that gave her an interesting, European air. "It's the mark of an educated person to study in Spain— you know, home of 'the pure Spanish—Castilian.' So what am I doing in *Catalan* Barcelona?" she joked.

"How did you learn English so well?

"I spoke English before I spoke Spanish—playing with kids from the U.S. from when I was tiny. You know, kids of ambassadors and the business world."

Of course I *didn't* know, but she went on. "So I really did learn to speak it before I knew much Spanish."

Vicky took a long draw on what was probably her third or fourth cigarette of the morning. A smoking friend no longer annoyed me. It seemed casual and comfortable.

In spite of all of her U.S. friends, she had not developed a love for big brother USA. "Everything in Bolivia is so dependent on the U.S. and its shitty capitalism," she complained, trying to impress me, I think, with how much U.S. slang she knew.

"Do you favor communism, then?" I asked.

"No, not really. Some type of socialism, I'm not sure what. You see, there are just two classes in Bolivia—upper and lower. No middle class. By luck I was born into the upper class."

She let that sink in. I wondered if she would be content to stay in the upper class when she returned to Bolivia. Would she be so vocal about the patronizing mentality of U.S. corporations when she was involved in a business career? I wondered these things, but didn't know her well enough to risk offense by sharing them with her.

"So what do you study?" she returned my question with genuine interest.

"Oh, I want to be a writer, I guess. Maybe a reporter for a newspaper. I'm not really sure."

"Then you should hear about. . . ." She gave me the name of a Barbara Walters-type journalist working in

Spain and the names of some literary magazines. We were both interested in art, photography, and a score of things we wanted to study if we had time.

It felt so good to converse on a deeper level than "pass the coffee" that I went around feeling wonderful the rest of the day, even though everyone else was feeling blue. All my friends were having "boyfriend problems." Guys weren't calling or weren't writing. In Nancy's case, two boyfriends were calling, writing, and sending wonderful care packages, leaving her totally confused.

"See what Dave sent me!" Nancy exclaimed, opening her latest package. "I wish he wouldn't do this! I can't believe what he spent just to get it here."

I blinked quietly. Mom and Dad hadn't even sent me a care package, let alone a guy.

"Here, Mel, have a cookie," Nancy tossed me one of the few that were still intact.

"And look, toilet paper! *Soft* toilet paper." She squeezed the package. "I'm not going to share this! He knows how I hate the 'sandpaper' here."

At the bottom of the box was a plain blue ski jacket.

"This is sweet, but I really don't need another jacket," Nan said, examining it. It was brand new. "Why don't you use it, Mel, till you buy the winter coat you keep talking about?"

"Oh, I couldn't take the gift Dave meant for you," I said. Nancy knew, though, that I was waiting for after-Christmas sales to buy a coat. Meanwhile, I was getting by with an old fake suede brown jacket I had bought at the Salvation Army.

"Dave won't mind. He's that generous. He probably

forgot he bought me a brand new one right before I left."

"Well, if you're sure," I said at last and tried the jacket on. "You're such a dear," I wanted, but wasn't able, to give her a hug.

A custom we all came to enjoy when we were feeling down was fixing café con leche in late afternoon. We would sop cookies in our mugs, soaking up each other's caring along with the coffee. We discussed Spanish stories we were reading, like "Castigo de Dios" (God's Punishment). This was a weird tale about cockroaches who were the only living things that survived nuclear war.

Some of the literature was surprisingly antiwar and even pacifist, but, as Arbonna had pointed out, obscure enough that it had gotten past the Spanish censors.

We also discussed weighty things like how fat we were getting. If only I could play basketball, my favorite sport. Then one day I spied a sign on a bulletin board about an intramural women's basketball game. I traveled across town by bus to a city gymnasium but found, not too surprisingly, nothing going on.

Nearby was another student. "Do you know anything about the women's basketball game that was supposed to be going on here today?" I asked.

"Well, yes, it was canceled," she answered in a friendly way. "Are you interested in basketball?"

"Oh, yes," I said, searching for Spanish. "In the U.S., I played on a team. Do you think I could here?"

"I'm sure you could. I go to the technical school, and we have a team that plays the other schools of the university. When the university starts in January, I'm sure you could play."

"Thank you, thank you very much," I said, as I found my way back to the bus stop. I felt warm all over, not just from the thought of getting to play basketball, but from having negotiated a Spanish conversation by myself.

I was still feeling good several days later when I went to Plaza Cataluña to meet another friend from our study group, nicknamed Odo, to go to a movie. Odo was a little late, but I never minded waiting in the plaza, watching little kids feed the pigeons, old men playing checkers, or couples strolling arm in arm. Would I ever be so lucky?

It was still warm for late November. From the port one could catch a faint whiff of sea breezes. Then a young man, about 23 or 24, walked up and started quizzing me in Spanish, *not* flirtatiously.

"Where are you from," he asked two or three times, while I debated whether I should talk to him.

"Germany? France?"

I refused to answer. Something about his manner made me feel strange.

"Where are you from?" he asked again, coming closer.

Finally, because I thought it would shut him up, I answered, "The United States." Immediately I knew it was the opening he was waiting for.

"Aha," he shot back. "*Many* states, but not very *united*, right?"

"Yes, I guess it's true," I sighed, thinking of Nixon, Watergate, and even the Vietnam War and the newly negotiated peace.

Then he proceeded to ask me something about Generalisimo Franco, a question I really didn't understand. Was he one of the spies Caman had warned us about, students who got you to bad-mouth Franco, then turned you in? I had always dismissed the warnings as farfetched. Caman had even shared the rumor that some students sat in classes at the university and informed against professors who were anti-Franco. Don't trust people who try to get you to talk about politics, we were told.

"I don't know. I don't know," I responded as he peppered me with a few more questions. Where was Odo? Why didn't she show up?

But I really didn't feel scared. I never did on the streets of Barcelona, even late at night. For one thing, there were few drunks in Spain, with wine a common but carefully handled feature of Spanish life. Rumor also had it that on the street, a woman could yell for the Guardia Civil. If she accused a man of bothering her, her word would automatically be accepted over his.

"What are you doing here, then?" he finally said, convinced he wasn't getting anywhere.

"I'm waiting for a girlfriend."

"Girlfriend? Better to be waiting for a boyfriend, no?" he said with a strange look as he started across the plaza.

I was never so happy to see a familiar face as when Odo arrived a few minutes later.

7

If I Can Just Survive Until Christmas

It wasn't long until I received a notice in the mail—a package awaited me at the post office. What could it be? Mom and Dad had hinted that they might go ahead and send a care package for Christmas, but it surely wouldn't be here already.

However, the post office was already closed for the day. I'd have to wait until after class the following day to retrieve it. I couldn't wait.

In a larger sense, most of us couldn't wait for Christmas either; it was the mooring from which we took hope. If I can survive until Christmas—the homesickness, frustration with language, wondering whether I'll get good enough grades—then I can surely get through the year, we told ourselves.

Several of us were flying to the States for Christmas, especially those who had special romances going. Others, like me, knew that parents or boyfriends were coming to Europe for the holidays. Nancy, two Inter-Varsity associates we had met, and I would go to Mittersill, Austria, for an Inter-Varsity conference held at a castle. Then I would travel alone to Rome, to meet my parents for New Year's. The holidays held high anticipation indeed.

The package, it turned out, was nothing but a cassette tape.

"Big deal," I told my roommates. "Here I thought maybe it would be 'goodies.' " I popped the cassette into the recorder.

"Hi, Mel," the familiar voice of my sister greeted me on the tape. "I'm terrible at writing letters. We thought we'd all sit here and talk to you." Pert! Just hearing her voice, chatting like she was sitting on my bed, made me blink back tears. My older sister, Nancy, had sent messages too, along with her little boy Larry. Their voices and love fed my spirit—and this care package wasn't even fattening.

Slowly the city began to put us in the mood for Christmas. Carols filled stores and lists crammed my pocketbook. My favorite haunts were the small shops in the Gothic quarter surrounding the old cathedral. These were the locally owned places where Barcelonians shopped, far from the gaudy tourist traps. The narrow, uneven brick streets always made me feel I was walking in the fourteenth instead of the twentieth century.

I was hurrying to catch the Metro one evening about 6:00, after shopping, when the clear hollow ring of the bell from the cathedral sent shivers to my bones. The only sounds were the bong, bong, bong, six times, from the cathedral, and off in the distance an animated discussion in Catalan.

I looked up at the lovely facade of the centuries-old

cathedral dominating the square and above that the perfect blue of an early December sky. Who had walked this plaza before me? There I stood, on the very stones where someone from the 1500s had stood, taking in scenery much as it had existed then. I was in love, smitten by the glamour of this ancient but cosmopolitan city.

All fall I had second-guessed myself, especially after Mom had sent word of a job offer from a Florida newspaper that had come shortly after I left. Why had I come? Was it God's will? What plans did God have for me in this year abroad?

That night in the plaza, I knew I didn't have to second-guess any longer. I was in the right place for this year. How could I even think of wishing I was Christmas shopping in malls at home! I *would* make it through the year, with God's help, and have peace doing it.

Yet there was so much I didn't know or begin to understand about the city, Spain, and Spaniards!

"When you look at an object," questioned Lydia, on one of the youth group's strolls after church at Calle Verdi, "do you think of the name of the object in Spanish or English?" We had been talking of my difficulty in mastering the language.

"Why, English, I guess, most of the time. Unless it's for something like café con leche. There's nothing exactly like café con leche in the U.S.," I said, laughingly.

"Well, to really see Spain through the eyes of a Spaniard," Lydia went on, "you have to expand your vocabulary. Find out the name of everything you see! Then, whenever you see that thing, name it in Spanish."

It sounded like a workable though time-consuming plan. "You may be right."

"Yes, and you will start thinking more like a Spaniard."

Strolls with the youth group, Bonnie said, were a must. Already she had deepening friendships with a number of the kids. The Spanish don't eat their mid-day meal till 1:30 or 2:00 p.m.—or even later on Sundays. So most of the kids would stroll blocks and blocks after church and then sit in a café and order drinks.

Cathy and I were always ravenous by the time we got out of church. We wanted to rush back to the residencia to prepare our own lunches since the seño-ra didn't serve any meals on Sunday.

"You have to go out more with the Spanish kids," Bonnie pleaded, and it wasn't just so she'd have other U.S. students along. Already her language skills had skyrocketed, from near bottom like me, to at home in Spanish, especially out of the classroom. I was im-pressed.

Bonnie would slip her arm naturally into the arm of one of the girls; off they'd go, Spanish-style. At first it felt awkward to me, but I wanted to look like the Span-ish girls (even though that was impossible). So Cathy and I would practice, like little kids trying out kissing, then collapse in giggles.

On the last day of classes before Christmas, the Camans invited the study group to their flat in the San Justo Desvern section of Barcelona. I always felt like I was in an art gallery at their place, with Mrs. Caman being an accomplished sculptor and Mr. Caman a not-bad painter.

"Does anyone know what we're having for supper?" Deb wondered as we made the long bus trip to their place.

"I think I heard Mrs. Caman say something about a chili supper," I replied. I remembered the delicious hamburgers they'd served the last time. Though strictly European in their own tastes, they knew how to cook what we were all hungry for, even if the results with Spanish ingredients were not quite "like Mother used to make."

"It's just so *great* not to worry about studying," Cathy sighed. "Can you believe we have a whole month off—almost to the middle of January?"

"Just think—we can stay out late, get up late. . . ."

"Are you guys going to Les Enfants after the party?" Deb wanted to know. She had started going to a popular disco with Tara on weekend nights. "They play really good U.S. songs there."

"I don't know," I hedged. I wanted to join the fun but didn't really know how to dance. It was one thing to flail your arms and legs around at an all-girl slumber party. It was quite another to try to dance at a real disco.

"Come on. You'll have fun, Mel, after our hard work," Deb went on. It was nice to feel included. After all, Deb could just go with Tara.

"Maybe," was all I promised.

The Camans had put up a Christmas tree. The chili was fantastic, and they had even bought little Christmas gifts for each of us. I was embarrassed that no one had even thought about giving the Camans anything; I guess we thought maybe they were too chic for all that. But they knew we were struggling with homesickness.

"Feliz Navidad," we called merrily as we left.

"Bon Nadal," someone returned in Catalan.

"Let's go to Les Enfants," said Joe, a tad too loudly from too much wine.

To cut out now seemed against the wonderful spirit of the night, a night for camaraderie after what was sometimes a tough, long fall.

"You coming, Mel?" Deb asked again.

"I will if you will," I said, turning to Cathy, not wanting to be goody-goody. I knew she thought a lot of Joe, and he was going. Of all the guys in the group, Joe was especially easy to talk to and usually interested in more than just partying.

"Oh, why not," Cathy agreed. "I'm up for a little celebrating."

"I'll see you guys later," Bonnie said, a touch of sadness in her big brown eyes. "I'm going home." A few others headed for separate destinations.

Les Enfants, short for the longer French name *Les Enfants Terribles*, reminded me of a leftover coffee house from the 60s. A low-hung wooden door made you slouch to enter, then you pulled aside a heavy, sound-proofing tarp to get in. To one side curled a long, high bar with a few swivel stools.

We all sat on benches awhile before a few got up to move to the hard rock sounds. "You have to kind of get into this place," Deb shouted, bouncing her head in time to the music. A strobe light made the dancers look like pieces of modern art. The beat was so strong it was impossible not to move.

"Come on," Deb pulled me to my feet. "It doesn't matter who dances with whom here. That's why we like it."

This seemed to be true. Definitely offbeat, with kids wearing T-shirts and jeans, or hamming it up in splashy clothes. One guy with a crazy loud tie and white pants glowed phosphorescently under the black light.

Slowly I began to move, closing my eyes so I wouldn't feel self-conscious. I needn't have bothered. Nobody was looking at me anyway. Nobody except Cathy knew I was a Mennonite who grew up believing that dancing was almost as bad as what dancing supposedly led to.

It felt almost like the first time I raised my hands in praise to the Lord—strange and awkward at first, then wonderfully freeing. I began to feel in touch with a new way of expressing happiness.

We sat down for a rest.

A man came around with a little tray. "What do you want to drink?" he asked.

"Oh, I don't care for anything," I said politely.

Deb punched me. "You have to order something. There's no cover charge to get in here, so they expect you to order something."

"But I don't even know the name of a drink," I said, embarrassed.

"Just order a Cuba Libre," Joe suggested.

The drink ordered, I asked Deb what it was.

"Oh, mostly Coke with a little rum."

Rum? I might have decided to have a little wine with meals, but rum?

By this time I was warm, though, and the cold drink tasted good. It was a little bit like strong cough medicine mixed with Coke. Going down it heated you up like cough medicine, too.

Getting up to dance was easier the next time. We soon moved around like the regulars, not really dancing with anyone in particular.

"I'm getting tired," Deb finally said around 1:00 a.m. "But I know Tara's not ready to go," Deb nodded in the Californian's direction. Tara had danced all night with her boyfriend. "Let's go back."

Deb, Cathy, Nancy, and I made our way back through the crowd and pulled back the tarp. The sudden lack of noise made the silence feel like you were deaf. But a sound to the right of us pulled us harshly back to reality. There stood Joe. He was spread-eagled, one hand holding himself from the wall of the building, retching and puking like a bum. He looked like the men I remembered seeing near the rescue mission when I was a child.

The evening's contents didn't look so chic when spilled on the street. Joe looked like he didn't want us to recognize him.

If God wanted me in Spain, did he want me in these bars, with kids who didn't profess much of anything? How could I be a presence here without being swept away by the fun and forbiddenness of it all? Was Bonnie doing the right thing? Or, by her quick, quiet departure from the group, was she cutting herself off from relating to these U.S. peers?

8

Storybook Christmas

Artists set up special stalls in front of the cathedral before Christmas to sell a huge variety of marvelously crafted nativity figurines. The morning after the party, I spent a good hour poring over the figures, until I had picked out a nice set to give to my parents. There was a little donkey with real sticks tied into bundles hanging on his sides, a tiny staff in the hand of a shepherd, and exquisitely detailed faces.

The vendor also talked me into buying a cheap, plastic "squatting Catalan."

"You take this, too," he said, smiling and pointing to the small pile of brown stuff back of the squatter's feet. "Give your friends in the United States a laugh."

Carefully I wrapped the figures in a discarded cookie box to carry to my Rome rendezvous with Mom and Dad two days after Christmas.

On December 21, Nancy and I joined Cindy and Nola (the two women we had met through the Inter-Varsity staff worker in Barcelona) on a 28-hour bus ride to Munich, Germany. There we would meet Nancy's boyfriend Mickey, before heading to the Austrian Alps by train for the Christmas conference.

"I don't know how I should act when I meet Mickey." Nancy was clearly excited. "He's only kissed me once."

"You're kidding."

"No, he's so old-fashioned it's hard to believe. But I love it. He's such a gentleman. Makes me feel so special."

"Take your cues from him, then," we all agreed.

I ended up sitting on the bus with a young Catalan student named Jorge. But he was hardly a country squatter.

"Where are you heading?" I asked. He had the high strong cheek bones of a German, blond curly hair, and I could tell by the way he had to scrunch up his knees in the seat that he was tall.

"I'm going to spend Christmas with relatives in Germany. My mom comes from Germany," he explained with a good-natured smile. "And you?"

"I'm going to the Alps."

"Oh, do you ski?"

"No, but I hope to learn this week."

That smile tugged at his face. Learn to ski in the Alps in one week, I supposed he was thinking.

"Do you ski?"

"Oh yes." He laid his head back in the seat. Living less than two hours from some of the best slopes in Northern Spain, he went often, he explained. And he was hoping to spend a lot of time skiing in Germany. Fantasies of enchanted evenings by chalet firesides filled my mind.

"Where are you going in the Alps?" he asked. Instinctively I could tell he was asking because this was going to be a long bus trip and we might as well pass the time enjoyably, not because of romantic interest in me.

"To a conference for Christian students, at a castle in the village of Mittersill," I told him, proud of actually conversing in Spanish.

"You're a Christian."

"Yes. Protestant."

"I'm a believer, too," he said simply. I was struck by the choice of words. I took it to mean that his faith actually meant something to him, that he was making an active choice to be a Christian, not just following a state-ordained faith.

"Oh really? What kind of church do you go to?"

"It's just a group of us. We're Catholics, but we've become disillusioned with the institutional church. We meet in homes and have discussions. We believe the state should be separate from religion, and that it's wrong to fight."

Jorge sounded more and more like an Anabaptist unaware.

"I can't believe it," I exclaimed, "I really didn't know there were Christians like you in Spain."

"Oh yes," he smiled. "There are a few of us." I told him about Mennonites, but that there weren't any Mennonite groups in Spain yet. I tried to explain the Anabaptist beginnings.

As the night wore on, I asked him questions—like was it really true that Protestants couldn't be buried in a Catholic cemetery? We spoke of Franco, of how to mix faith and social action, and about the car bomb assassination of President Carrero Blanco the night before. Blanco had apparently been the victim of a Basque terrorist attack. Barcelona had seemed like a police state, with police on every corner.

Gradually conversation was replaced by long silences. I let my head fall to his shoulder as a prop. But I had to recognize it was only a brotherly gesture when he let his head rest on mine.

In the morning, I sheepishly thanked him for letting me use his shoulder. He grinned. I had just spent a very innocent night with a strange man!

When the bus stopped for gas in Germany, a Japanese guy asked me in French if I spoke French. I said no, but that I spoke Spanish and English.

He sighed and switched to English. "Maybe you can help me anyway. I can't figure out how to use this German phone."

"Hey, I met a guy on the bus who knows German well." I motioned for Jorge to come over. "I'm sure he can help you." Jorge could easily read the instructions on the phone but couldn't communicate them to our new friend, since they didn't have a common language.

"Why doesn't Jorge get on the phone with the German operator," I told each of them. "Jorge can tell me in Spanish what to do. I'll tell you in English, and we'll go back and forth that way till we get through!"

"Our own little U.N." we said, laughing when the call went through.

As Munich neared, I found myself not wanting the ride with Jorge to be over. But I was relieved to be almost through a 28-hour trip.

"What is your address?" he asked as we left the bus. I was sure it would end up like so many exchanged addresses—yellow and dog-eared in a wallet. Then he surprised me by kissing me softly on the cheek.

"Nothing will come of it," I reminded myself, marveling to find one man in Spain who wasn't on the make.

Mickey was at the bus station. Nancy and he exchanged a restrained hug that surely didn't reflect their true feelings. I was happy to meet him, too, after hearing so much about him all fall. He really was as tall as Nancy said, and just as teddy-bearish.

"This is *all right*," Nola exclaimed as we headed out on the Munich streets to find a student hostel. "A West Point officer for an escort!"

"Isn't it great?" Nancy's cheeks glowed bright red like they always did when she was happy. Mickey took her hand.

Sunday morning was the kind postcards are made of, so we headed for the deserted Olympic village where little more than a year earlier Mark Spitz had earned his seven gold medals before terrorists fulfilled everyone's worst nightmares. We walked around silently, remembering all the spots we had seen on television, finally pausing for an impromptu worship service on a hill.

The train for Mittersill left that afternoon. From the train station, a van ferried us to the castle high on the side of a mountain overlooking the village.

I kept pinching myself, especially when I got to my room. Most of the girls stayed in rooms with six or eight bunks. Since I was leaving early, they gave me a tiny room all to myself, at the top of the castle. I even had my own bathroom, the only time I was so blessed in all Europe.

A gigantic down tick covered my tiny bed. As I snuggled under its warmth, I was glad I hadn't gone home for the holidays. I might spend the rest of my life in a three-bedroom, ranch-style house, but for three nights I would be queen of a castle, a castle with a real dungeon and lookouts in the towers.

·"Do you think it seems like Christmas?" Nancy had asked at supper that evening. "This is the first Christmas I've been away from home."

"I know. Me too," I said. "I think I'm going to call home on Christmas Day even though I'll see Mom and Dad two days later."

"I'm just so glad you could come up here," Nancy went on. "It's wonderful to have Mickey here, but you don't want to be somewhere at Christmas where you know only one person."

I nodded. "You know what I'll miss? This year my family decided to have a pig roast on Christmas Day!"

"Your family sounds so neat," Nancy said. "I can't wait to meet your mom and dad."

"You think *you* can't wait to meet them? I've been writing all fall about this wonderful Nancy and Cathy and. . . ."

"I just wish you didn't have to travel to Italy by yourself."

"Oh, I'll be fine," I said, with more confidence than I felt. "In fact, I'm kind of looking forward to seeing if I can do it all by myself."

"Yeah, but if you're late or something, what will your parents do?"

"Worry." We both laughed.

The Christmas conference was a gathering point for international students from all over Europe. It was fun to be able to sympathize, in a new way, with the non-English kids who were trying to speak English, and swap tales and problems with other U.S. students studying abroad.

One thing bothered me. Most of the students, myself included, were from a middle-to-upper-income group, as shown by our ability to study abroad. How could I justify spending money on a castle hideaway when . . . (and Dad's facts and figures on starving people came floating to mind).

On Christmas Eve, after a hearty soup, black bread, and wonderful cheeses, the entire conference group boarded buses to attend a worship service at a little Lutheran church in the village. Outside the church, we gathered around a Christmas tree that had *real* candles on it and sang carols. The Austrians began filling the church, smiling broadly as we sang. At last, clear-toned bells rang out in the approaching dusk.

It was too much. Again I blinked back tears, tears for the beauty of it all, for the magic of being here, so close to my spiritual and biological ancestors. And for the wonderful new Christian friends, of more nationalities than I could count—Austrians, Germans, French, Dutch, English, U.S., Canadians, Africans, Japanese, Italians, Australian, New Zealanders.

In the service, little kids in bright stocking caps sing-songed their Christmas pieces. A minister delivered a Christmas homily in German. If I closed my eyes, it wasn't too hard to imagine a Martin Luther or Conrad

Grebel or Menno Simons preaching. Singing "Silent Night" in German, not for fun but because it was the real local language, I wept.

I wept also because I knew I was about as close to heaven on earth as one gets, what with all the stripes and colors of people around me, including an infinite variety of theological persuasions. Who needs biological family when a Christian family surrounds you?

Christmas afternoon I climbed a hill behind the castle and tried to etch the ancient Alps, their tops mixed up with clouds, on my mind. The clouds were engaged in their own game of tag in the late afternoon sun. I soared around, singing like Maria in *Sound of Music*. Then I watched the valley below get dark, while I still sat high in sun. On the other side of the world, my parents would just be waking to Christmas morning. Here it was already gone, but Mom and Dad would soon race against the sun to join me.

If Christmas is only presents, family, food, and doing the things you've always done, then no, it *didn't* seem like Christmas that year. But if Christmas is celebrating God taking on flesh, God entering our lives as Emmanuel, then surely it was my best Christmas.

As I let it sink in that God, Creator of the universe, Creator of the awesome Alps, truly entered into our world in Jesus, I knew I had found the true meaning of Christmas. Perhaps it was good to be away from the usual tinsel and traditions to see if there was still something left. The real test, though, would be to celebrate Christmas in a situation less storybookish than an Alpine holiday—like a Calcutta sidewalk.

It was a thought that would carry me through some dark hours just ahead.

9

Roman Adventure

It was still dark, early on the morning of December 26, when the van from the castle left me at the train station in Mittersill. All the signs were in German. The only person in the station at that hour spoke German.

If only Cathy were here, I thought. Or Jorge, or my dad who at least knew Pennsylvania Dutch—low German. Why had I thought I could manage by myself in a country where I barely knew two words? How did I think I would get myself to Rome, find a hotel, and manage to meet my parents in a strange airport?

The travel agency in Mittersill had written on a piece of paper exactly what train I should take and when it left. I showed it to the attendant. He nodded his head, shuffled over to a blackboard, and pointed to the train listed under what I assumed said "Departures." The name matched that on my scrap of paper. I gave him the last of my Austrian schillings and clutched my ticket.

Slowly a few other passengers carting skis joined me on the platform. It was frigid high in these Alps. A

73

light hurtled out from between the mountains, whistling to a stop. I gathered up my suitcase, purse, and satchel holding my lunch. Then I lumbered back the hallway that ran alongside the train's compartments. At last, an empty one.

I checked the guidebook for Rome, poring over Italian phrases. It would be at least 11:00 p.m. when I got to Rome. Would Rome feel as safe as Barcelona at night? Would there be a place open to get Italian money right away? I wondered if Mom and Dad were getting up yet for their trip. There was no backing out now.

There seemed to be a number of cheap *pensiones*, homes which rented out rooms for the night, within a few blocks of the station. I found one address and rang the bell. A woman's voice came over the speaker. Yes, she had rooms, at about $6 apiece.

"I'll take one," I said, not hesitating.

As soon as I met my hostess, I knew I had made the right choice. The room was attractive, clean, and cozy, with a bathroom right down the hall. A bed never felt so good.

At last it was time to go to the airport, time to meet my parents for whom I had been so homesick all fall. I had been apart from them only as long as a normal term away at college. But somehow the ocean between us had made it different.

At the airport, I found my way to the place persons come out of customs. Before I knew it, they were with me, all of us hugging and crying in a crazy mob. Dad looked distinguished, with a new beard, but Mom appeared dreadfully tired.

74

"Let's go get our luggage," Dad said, before we'd finished hugging.

"So how was your trip?" I asked.

"Oh, okay," Mom replied. "I just forgot how long it takes to fly to Europe. And we aren't getting younger."

"Did you find us a hotel?" Dad wanted to know.

"Well, not really. I thought we'd do that together."

"Well where did *you* stay last night?"

"Oh, you wouldn't want to stay there. It was just a little pensione—like a boarding house. But I've got the names of some cheap hotels."

"Well, it doesn't have to be too cheap," Dad smiled. "Remember, this is our anniversary trip."

"Speaking of cheap, I can't believe you're still wearing that coat from the Salvation Army," Mom said. "Don't you have anything better?"

"It's warm enough." I shrugged. Mom was probably a little embarrassed to be seen with me. I smiled to myself, feeling wonderfully loved and critiqued at the same time.

We boarded the airport bus to downtown Rome, straining to catch glimpses of famous landmarks. I tried to decipher Italian signs while Dad bragged to anyone who would listen that this was his daughter, studying in Spain for the year.

"Are you a professor?" the hotelkeeper asked Dad.

"No, no," Dad laughed. "I'm a farmer."

The hotelman appealed to Mother. "His beard makes him look like a professor of philosophy, don't you think?"

Mom let out her trademark laugh. "I guess so!"

I soon lost track of days and time. We floated along

in a tourist world of hotels, restaurants, sightseeing, and not having worries more major than taking the right bus.

The Colosseum, the Forum, St. Peter's Square, more basilicas than we cared to count, the Sistine Chapel. There was time enough to explore the famous and the not so famous, and to stumble across flea markets and hidden restaurants that were a delight to the eye as well as to the tongue.

"If this hotel just weren't so cold, everything would be fine," Mom complained. Rome in late December had a raw, biting dampness that chilled you on the streets. The space heaters in our rooms didn't help much. We had other typical tourist complaints of indigestion, diarrhea/constipation, callouses, and high prices. And I had thought it was just college kids or younger who were experts at complaining!

Soon we really had something to complain about. We boarded a crowded bus to ride out to the Catacombs of St. Sebastian, along the Appian Way.

"Just grab a ring and get off at the Basilica of St. Sebastian," I shouted to Mom and Dad, who looked helpless. We couldn't even stand near each other on the bus. At the next stop even more people crowded on, so that everyone was body to body. Slowly I became aware that the man behind me seemed to be pushing even closer. What was he up to? Up and down he rubbed his front against my backside. Suddenly I was sick. Pervert!

I was locked in by people on every side, no way to move one inch. What could I do? Even parents in the same bus couldn't protect me now.

76

As we neared our stop, I yelled to Mom and Dad, "Get off here." The bus lurched to a stop. Gathering all the strength and momentum I could in the crowded bus, I raised my right heel forward, then shoved it backward against the shin of the offending passenger. Bam!

I'm sure that it hurt, but I never heard a whimper as I escaped out the open door.

"Mom," I said, with an involuntary shudder. "You'll never guess what happened on that bus."

"*You'll* never guess what happened to me," she said, her brown eyes cold and hard.

"There was this man, rubbing himself. . . ."

Then Mom laughed. "There was this man behind *me*. . . ."

"Good grief!" I said. "It's one thing with a twenty-two-year-old college kid. But a fifty-nine-year-old grandmother?" Dad looked embarrassed, for his wife, his daughter, his gender.

"I kicked him good as we got off," I chuckled. "It had to have hurt, but I didn't hear a thing. Not very pacifist, was I?"

Dad grunted, his usual sermon about "turning the other cheek" not quite appropriate now!

The catacombs were impressive but creepy. "Can you imagine having prayer meetings in these rooms?" I marveled.

"There are many Christian martyrs buried here," Dad said. Suffering and dying for one's faith suddenly seemed much closer than it had before, making my struggles about how to live my faith seem superficial.

Dad wanted to buy a postcard to send our pastor at

home. "My traveler's checks are gone!" he whispered, all color draining from his farmer's tan.

"But how can you still have your wallet?" Mom asked. "Maybe the checks fell out in the catacombs."

They sent a guide back with Dad to look, while Mom and I fretted.

"At least I have my credit cards and cash," Dad said reappearing. "Someone must have cleverly lifted out just the checks. At least we had American Express." It sounded like a commercial but no one laughed. The vacation was clearly over.

He pondered when he had last used his wallet. "My pocket must have been picked on that *bus!*" He spat out the word like a curse.

"We certainly got our fill of 'Roman' hands on that bus," Mom joked, always one to try to smooth things over.

"I guess we'll kill tomorrow tracking down the American Express office and stuff," Dad said, taking charge again. We had enough money to tide us over supper and next morning. I was so thankful it hadn't happened to me when I was alone.

After we had gotten replacement checks next morning, we bought tickets for an expensive excursion to the island of Capri the following day. A sightseeing bus took us south to Naples, then we took a ferry to the island, where the rich and famous were rumored to cavort.

A funny and nice-looking guide made the trip lots of fun, and a good mix of people from many countries kept conversation interesting. We ate lunch with a Japanese student at a beautiful four-star hotel overlooking the bay.

"Can you believe how blue the water is?" I marveled.

"Doesn't it remind you of Oregon's Crater Lake?" Mom remembered. We never were wealthy, but somehow, as they had for this trip, Mom and Dad always scraped money together. Capri would now enter that memory bank which holds only the crystal blue of the sea, not mundane things like restroom lines.

On the trip back to Rome, we sat near the front of the bus and the guide struck up conversation with Mom and Dad. He seemed to be originally from France and spoke five or six languages.

"Our daughter is living in Barcelona this year, so we thought we'd take advantage of it to visit Spain and Italy," Dad said.

"Oh, so you speak Spanish," the guide turned to me.

"Sí," I said with a grin.

"Let's talk Spanish, then."

"Okay with me," I nodded. "I'm kind of getting out of practice anyway, with all this traveling over the holidays."

"Where have you traveled?"

I thought back to the bus trip to Munich, which now seemed as far away as high school. I could already tell this guide's intentions were different than Jorge's. I kind of liked it. It had been so long since I'd had a real date, since I'd felt wanted. What kind of man was he, anyway?

"How would you like to celebrate New Year's Eve with me?" he asked, still in Spanish.

I looked over at Mom and Dad. They, of course hadn't caught a word, not even the drift. They were lost in the sweetness of each other's company.

"I don't know," I hedged.

"They'd like to be by themselves for one evening," he kept pushing. Could I trust him? He looked at least thirty. A real Italian New Year's Eve celebration!

"I'll take you back to your hotel by 1:00 a.m. or so," he went on. "No big deal. What do you think?"

I looked at Mom and Dad again. Would it be safe? At least Mom and Dad had met him. They'd probably approve. I was long past the age of asking their permission for a date anyway.

"No, I don't think so," I finally said, giving him a big smile so he wouldn't think I didn't like him. "I don't think I should go out with a strange man. Besides, I'm tired."

"Too big of day," he stated, suddenly just guide and tourist again. Soon we were back in Rome.

"Thank you for the lovely trip," Mom said.

"You are quite welcome," answered the guide politely. Then in Spanish he asked me once more, "Sure you won't go out with me?"

"No, I'd better go home. But thanks. I had a good time too."

Once out of earshot, I told Mom and Dad about the invitation. "Do you think it would have been okay to go?"

"So that's what was going on," Mom smiled. "It would probably have been okay, but I'm glad you didn't. Have you had any dates this year?" Mom asked. She never tried to pry, but, of course, she was curious.

"No. . . ."

"I wouldn't have asked, but so many people ask me if you have a Spanish boyfriend."

"Tell them not to hold their breath."

I ordered breakfast in bed for Mom and Dad the next morning, their anniversary.

"You know," Mom exclaimed, as we prowled around later looking for open spots on New Year's Day, "I haven't had my headaches on this trip."

"And my back isn't bothering me," Dad added. "I think this vacation is good for us." For their anniversary supper we found a delightful restaurant in the Trastevera section of the city. We enjoyed a strolling violinist, candles, and the waiter even brought out a special Italian "cake" when he heard it was an anniversary.

"A most memorable anniversary," Mom sighed when we got back to the hotel.

"Why don't you go and take a nice long, hot bath," Dad suggested to me. Suddenly I caught *his* drift. How unfortunate to share a room with your kid on your anniversary!

The bathroom was down the hall away from the hotel room but otherwise quite comfortable. I never spent a happier bathtime! Would I ever find love as true and faithful and holy as Mom and Dad's? Surely waiting for such love was worth giving up the chance for a romantic night in Rome with a dashing stranger.

Too soon came the day of our departure. Dad always likes to arrive extra early at airports, so we were there in plenty of time to check in. I went with him to the registration desk.

"Miller. Miller. . . . I'm sorry, we don't have reservations for any *Miller*," said the polite attendant in good but accented English.

81

"What do you mean?" said Dad. "Our tickets here say 'Alitalia, Flight 687, 11:30.'"

"I'll look again." She checked one list, then another. "I'm sorry, Mr. Miller, we simply don't have a reservation for you."

"That is ridiculous! What are we supposed to do? We have to get to Barcelona!"

"Well, I can let you go standby. *If* there are seats."

"How does it look now? Is it full?"

"Yes, it is full. But there may be cancellations. No shows."

"For three?"

"Well, that's doubtful," she agreed. "But we'll try."

Dad turned around with a look on his face like a tornado had just devastated his corn crop. "I can't believe this," he mustered. "Of all the stupid. . . ." Then he caught himself. Never one to engage in stereotypes, he had almost disparaged the entire Italian race because of two molesters, one pickpocket, and one failed airline reservation.

It was 11:15, then 11:20. Dad went back to the desk. "Don't you have any seats for standbys? We've got to get on that plane." The clerk shook her head, now busy with last minute check-ins.

We could hear the calls for boarding. How would we ever make it to the gate in time?

"Jeepers!" was the strongest word Daddy allowed himself. My stomach was tied in a pretzel. Mom looked like she had a headache. They couldn't just leave us stranded in Rome, could they?

"They just overbooked, and she doesn't want to admit it," Dad fumed. "Our name has to be there."

The clock showed 11:25, then 11:30. Suddenly the whole departure area got quiet. People stopped rushing. The clerk turned around to remove the little sign announcing our flight from the "Departures" sign.

We just looked at each other, too angry to cry. The plane had gone. We obviously were not on it. What could we do now?

"I can book you tomorrow," she said.

"Don't you owe us hotel vouchers?"

"No, your names weren't on the reservation list."

"How will we be sure our names will be there tomorrow?" Dad asked.

"I'm booking you right now."

"I want to speak to your manager," Dad demanded.

"You can go to the airline office, upstairs to the right."

No one was there.

"I guess we just get on the bus and go back to Rome and find another hotel," I choked back tears. Who wanted to see anything else in Rome? Barcelona was where I was supposed to be heading, the pearl on the other side of the Mediterranean, a jewel I now longed to show off to my parents. The happy chatter that had filled our first trip on this bus into Rome hung like a distant, tainted memory.

Dad went to bed as soon as we found a room, even though it was only four in the afternoon.

"Don't you want to go out for supper with us?" Mom asked.

"Not hungry."

"Shall we bring you something?"

"Oh, maybe some crackers or fruit. I just want to get out of this city."

We did some disinterested window-shopping. Then we decided if Dad wasn't with us, the least we could do was eat pizza, since Dad didn't like that. Entirely different than any pizza I ever had, it tasted wonderful. It was a little solace for the big disappointment of the day.

When I heard that terrorists exploded a bomb in that same airport some three weeks later, I knew again the truth that no matter how bad things get, they could have been worse.

10

"Spanish" Student

The return to Barcelona the next day was anti-climactic. But somehow it was fitting that, when I went to pick up my luggage, my soft-sided tote bag had been badly torn in transit.

"One more souvenir from Alitalia," Dad scoffed. He was unwilling at that point to look up the airline office to make a damaged luggage claim.

Mom and Dad enjoyed seeing the flat farmlands on the outskirts of the city and wondering what crops grew there. I couldn't help but think about the last time I had traveled that route, back in August when I was excited, green, and scared. Now I felt experienced and worldly-wise, showing off to my parents the city I had come to love.

Christmas wasn't really over in Barcelona. In fact, shopping for the gift-giving Day of the Three Kings, January 6, was in full swing.

"I can't believe all the Christmas lights you have here," Mom and Dad marveled. That Christmas in the States everyone had been encouraged to conserve electricity because of the oil crisis.

Having Mom and Dad see my home and meet Conchita, the caretaker, was high priority. "I want you to meet my parents," I said proudly to Conchita, in Spanish.

"Mucho gusto," Conchita returned. "Melodie is a good boarder." I translated.

"Oh she's always been a good girl," Daddy chimed in.

I tried to translate that without sounding boastful. It felt funny to actually know more Spanish than someone else. My new role as translator helped me feel talkative and adventuresome with the language.

"I will soon have someone for you to meet, too," Conchita beamed. "When the university starts, you will have a Spanish girl for a roommate, maybe two."

"That's great!" I replied. Conchita knew how much we had been wanting Spanish roommates. She also knew the *Americanas* had a tendency to keep to themselves and chatter in English.

One of the excursions I planned for my parents was an hour's trip outside Barcelona to Monserrat, a mountain that because of the unusual shapes of its stones was revered as holy. An order of monks had a monastery there. The only way up was a thrilling cable car ride, about as cut off from the world as anyone could live.

It was a sky-blue perfect day. We enjoyed picnicking in the mountains and getting back to nature after nearly two weeks of asphalted cities.

"This is beautiful, but how can these monks think they're serving God, so removed from the 'world'?" I mused.

"You've got me," Mom chimed in. "All these statues and shrines. . . ." She shivered. "A little too close to idolatry, if you ask me."

"Of course, we have our own idols." I needn't have reminded them. "And it would be easier to be really dedicated to God up here—no distractions. They have plenty of time to read and meditate and pray."

We agreed we shouldn't judge those who feel God has called them to a life of practicing the spiritual disciplines. Certainly the mystics have contributed much to Christian thought. That didn't make the lifestyle easier to understand, though.

"This helps me be even more grateful for the early Anabaptist leaders," Dad reflected. "Some left the priesthood partly for this very reason: how do you serve God when you live separate from the world?"

"Yet separatism was what they preached, too," I exclaimed, remembering from studies that they would have no part of earthly systems, like military protection from the king. That meant literally being "like sheep among wolves."

My mind was in a philosophical frame that day, and perhaps God really did speak to me on the holy mountain. What was all this saying? What did God want me to do in the world? How could I live in the world, yet be separate from it? Mom and Dad were quiet too, pondering questions with which Christians in all centuries and cultures must struggle.

It was late by the time I had accompanied Mom and Dad back to their hotel.

"Don't you think we ought to go with you?" Mom asked politely, as I prepared to head back to the residencia.

"Of course not, I'll be fine. I go anywhere by myself, even late at night in this town."

It was wonderful to feel so safe in a city, and ironic that one enjoyed this freedom in a land where other freedoms were routinely suppressed.

Thoughts of Monserrat were still on my mind as I went down in the subway station. An old woman was sweeping up the results of a day's carelessness—litter, cigarette butts, newspapers. Here was the real world! Here was someone serving humanity. The only time sweepers could clean the stations was late at night. What a lonely, unappreciated job!

The air was full, too, of exhaust fumes and the peculiar, unforgettable stench of an underground transportation system. The woman was so bent and in black widow's garb. I almost cried thinking of her working night after night in such an atmosphere.

What would she think if I went up to her and thanked her for her work? Probably that I was trying to rob her or was a spy. If there were only some way to express my appreciation, to treat her as a human being. For if I didn't, I might as well be living up on a holy mountain somewhere, aloof and uninvolved in the world.

When I got to my stop and was leaving the station, another old woman was trying to get out the door, half bent over with bags and packages. She was probably going home from her shift at sweeping. I hurried to open it for her; her smile sent an unspoken thank you.

Here was one thing I could do without having my intentions misinterpreted. It was a tiny, insignificant gesture to be sure, but it helped me be glad to walk the tightrope of "being in the world, but not *of* it," rather than opting for isolation.

Too soon it was time to take Mom and Dad to the Barcelona airport. "I don't think I'll be so homesick anymore," I smiled, trying—and failing—to put all my emotions into words. "I just can't thank you enough for spending the money to come, and all the things we got to do, and all you got for me over here."

Dad rummaged in his pocket and brought out all his Spanish coins, then also took Spanish bills from his wallet. He shoved them into my hand.

"Don't you think you ought to exchange them back to dollars?" I stammered.

"They'll lose too much value changing them back again. You just keep it—an extra Christmas present."

"But, Dad," I cried. Yet I knew the matter was closed. "I'm sure it will come in handy. I won't blow it."

Then all that was left to Mom and Dad's long-awaited visit was one last hug, one last "take care," and they were gone. They disappeared in a crowd down the hall.

"You sure have fun parents," Deb said that night, as we tried to prepare ourselves for the first real classes next day.

"Yeah, they're pretty great most of the time," I agreed. Even in college it wasn't wise to appear to like your parents too much.

"How do you get along so well?" Deb wondered.

"Oh, I guess I've just always toed the line. I'm sure you wouldn't think they were fun if I was over here smoking grass or something."

Deb grinned. She often looked like she was enjoying a secret joke. "Yeah, I suppose your mom would loose her cool, like mine did when she found birth control pills in my purse."

"Really. That wouldn't go over so good." I tried not to look surprised. That must mean she sleeps with her boyfriend, like Tara, I thought.

"Well it didn't with my mom, either. She got really mad."

I knew this was not the time to preach.

"I enjoyed having Mom and Dad here, but I'm anxious to get into our classes now."

"I'll remind you of that in about two months," Deb laughed. It felt good to see Deb again. She really was a friend, in spite of a world of differences.

"So how was Larry?" I asked.

"Great. Looking really good. I spent a couple of days at Bridgewater College with him before I came back here. And I got to see all my friends."

"Wish you were back at school there?"

"Naw, not really. I mean it was fun to have everyone asking me how's Spain, and to think about coming back here to start our real classes."

"Yeah, I just hope I'm not completely lost."

"Really! Me too."

"Huh? You don't have to worry. You talk Spanish like a—"

"Sure, sure. We'll see."

It turned out I didn't even have to worry about such questions the first day. Most of the professors arrived at least twenty minutes late. Students straggled into class as late as forty minutes. Throughout the class, kids chain-smoked, making the lecture halls as blue as any bar.

But the last straw for me was that the professors, instead of handing out typed course outlines and bibliographies, dictated them to us. Like a roomful of secretaries, we wrote down titles, authors, and names of publishers as fast as we could.

The other surprise of the day was realizing that most of the students were also studying in a language that was not their native tongue. Almost all were Catalan, including the professors, yet they were forced by law to conduct classes in Spanish.

I had signed up for one class with Dr. Arbonna. His contact with U.S. teachers and systems showed when he was the lone prof to show up with a neatly-typed course syllabus and bibliography.

The next trick was scouring the bookstores around the university to find the texts we needed. The books seemed inexpensive compared to texts in the States—but cheaply made, with rough, ragged edges and some pages uncut.

In one tiny shop, the owner spent almost an hour talking to me in Spanish. He was a writer, he said, but none of his books had been published because they were too risky—with political and religious themes. He kept stopping to ask if I understood him. Marvel of marvels, I did!

As promised, Spanish roommates had moved in with us by that evening. Our new roommate was named "Conchita," just like the landlord of the residencia, meaning "little shell." It was a popular name in Spain.

She was a tall Catalan, with dark hair swinging in a pony tail, pretty and friendly and studying to be a pharmacist. Of course, she smoked, so my clothes soon smelled like everyone else's. I had to get used to seeing a dirty ashtray sitting on the table in our room.

That weekend Conchita invited Deb and me to go with her to meet some of her friends downtown at a "bohemian" (Conchita's description) little place. It was wonderful to be finally forced to talk in Spanish. Ironically, Conchita and her friends kept having to remind themselves to talk in Spanish too, instead of slipping back into Catalan.

Later, Conchita left her friends, and the three of us from the residencia went to Les Enfants till about 9:30.

"Let's go to Wimpys," Deb said, "I'm starved."

"Hey," called some U.S. sailors when we were out on the street, mistaking all of us for "home" girls.

"Hola," Deb returned, like she didn't understand English—but also for the benefit of Conchita.

"Wanna come get high with us?" the sailor went on.

"No entiendo [I don't understand]," replied Deb.

We hurried off, suppressing laughs. Even Conchita understood enough to know what had transpired.

Classes began to be surprisingly easy. So many of the words used in formal instruction had a Latin base that was often similar to an English equivalent. The one class I thought would be a breeze because it was taught in English—English poetry—turned out to be the toughest. That was because most of my classmates were graduate students who knew much more about English poetry than I did. And it was taught by an exacting English woman who accepted only the best.

"I've just got to see if I can get a library card," I told Cathy one night. "This English class is pushing me to my limit. I need to find some of the books she was recommending."

"Let's check out the library tomorrow," Cathy agreed. After an hour and a half of chasing red tape, Cathy was ready to pull her hair out, but we finally got the precious cards.

Then we discovered that you couldn't just walk to the shelves and pull off any book you wanted. You had to submit a requisition for one and have a helper retrieve it. If it wasn't what you needed, you then sent it back and got another one. Frustration! Why had we bothered to come to Spain to study when we spent so much time battling systems rather than studying?

"I just don't think I'm getting a very good education this year," Cathy said that evening, sighing.

"Really!" I chimed in. "I think many of the kids in my classes know more than the professors."

"All they ever do is read from books, calling it 'commentary on the text'. "

"Yeah, it got to be a little too much the other day when my 'Generation of 27' professor read a book to us in French, translated it to Spanish, then I had to translate to English in my head!" I added.

"The professors aren't paid much," Conchita confided. "That's why they can't get anyone very good. Now you know why Spanish students are demonstrating all the time."

"I'm *beginning* to understand," I said. "We're kind of uninvolved—like spectators, because we know after a year we're leaving. But if I were a student here all the time it would be *really* frustrating."

"It's the only thing they can do—demonstrate," Cathy agreed.

"Do you think there will be more closings, now that the university is finally opened?" Deb asked.

"I don't know." Conchita dropped her voice. "I've heard rumors—"

"I saw some posters on the walls by the student café again," said Cathy. "But they're always written in Catalan, so I don't really understand them."

"At least I see now *why* I don't understand them," I added. "I used to think it was Spanish words I hadn't learned yet!" Everyone laughed.

"It must be very hard for you, with all of us talking Catalan all the time." Conchita looked guilty.

"Oh, but Catalan is such a beautiful language—I don't mind at all when you talk it with your friends. We're picking up more all the time. Aren't we, Deb?"

"Really!" Deb said. "I couldn't believe it the other day when I followed practically a whole conversation."

Conchita grinned. Now we were actually talking Spanish so much that our tongues got physically tired, from twisting themselves in ways not natural to us.

"I'm looking forward to spending the day at Ruth's on Saturday," Cathy said to me later, as we washed up in the residencia bathroom.

Barcelona's Inter-Varsity Christian Fellowship director, Ruth, had asked us to come to sort of a seminar on "evangelism as it applies to the Spaniard" that she was conducting at her apartment.

"Yeah, I'm sure we'll have a great meal," I said. "But I just don't know about this evangelism bit. I'm so afraid of turning people off to God. Like Deb and Tara. Agnostics. What can we possibly say to them?"

"Well, I don't know," Cathy countered, "but I think

Ruth's right when she says that since there are so few real Christians in Spain, we really do have a reason for being here besides studying."

The seminar was excellent. When I found out that Ruth had grown up a General Conference Mennonite, it made me feel more at home with her. She talked about the special problems and questions that come up when talking to Catholics about a personal relationship with Jesus Christ.

"Forget about us talking to Spanish students," I blurted out, finally saying what had been on my mind. "We don't even know what to say to our U.S. roommates, who think there's no way to know for sure there is a God!"

Ruth smiled. "Maybe you could start a Bible study at the residencia—an objective, academic look at the claims of Christ, studying whom he said he was."

My heart started pounding just like it always did when I knew someone was speaking the truth but I didn't want to hear it. A Bible study with Deb and Tara! We simply couldn't.

When we got back to the residencia, I was glad that Conchita was the only one in the room. "Did you have a nice time today?" she inquired politely.

"Um, yes," I said, yawning as I got ready for bed.

"What did you do?"

"Well, a woman was telling us how to, how to tell others about God," I stammered.

"Oh, that's interesting." Conchita replied. "Everyone in Spain knows about God, but, of course, not very many are practicing."

I nodded. "That's the point. She wasn't wanting us

to convert Catholics, but to help others know Jesus in a personal way."

"Speaking of Jesus . . ." Conchita said. "Why don't Protestants believe in the complete virginity of Mary?

"What do you mean?" I asked.

"Well, you say Jesus had brothers and sisters, so Mary couldn't have remained a virgin all her life."

Why couldn't Conchita have started with an easier question?

"That's a good question," I said, smiling. "I didn't really know Catholics didn't think Jesus had brothers and sisters."

"And why don't you follow the Pope's authority? Jesus gave the Pope authority through Peter."

I was silent.

"Do you think unbaptized children go to hell?"

So Ruth was right. Talking about one's faith in Spain did carry special dimensions. All I could tell Conchita was that I couldn't answer the questions in Spanish, but that I'd look up some things and we'd talk again.

"I'd definitely be interesting in learning more," Conchita finished, which was the opening I needed.

"Well, we were talking about starting a Bible study here at the residencia," I said, delighted that here was one person expressing interest in a Bible study even before it was planned.

I snuggled into bed that night content to know, once again, that surely I was in the place God wanted me to be that year. My sleep was sweet and long.

11

"Pagan"

Eventually a second roommate, Concha (a different form of the name *Conchita*), moved in to our suite with its four cots. For several weeks, we made a happy foursome. Deb and I learned to survive our hunger pangs for supper until 8:00 or 9:00 in the evening, when our Spanish roommates were accustomed to eating. On the one-burner camp stove Cathy bought, we'd make soup from dry mixes and *tortillas*—which in Spain meant omelets filled with mushrooms, potatoes, sausage, or even artichoke.

It was fascinating to listen to Concha and Conchita carry on in Catalan, a language with funny slurs and tones that almost sounded like one had too much saliva in the mouth. Smoking was as much a part of the daily meal as coffee.

"I think I'll take up smoking," Deb said, testing me.

"Well, our clothes already reek. . . ." I shrugged.

"Concha's friends can't believe I don't smoke," she went on.

"I know. It's like we're from another planet if we don't."

"It's not like I have to keep smoking when I get back to the States or anything," Deb continued, now arguing with herself. "And it will keep me from gaining more weight."

I just shrugged. Smoking now seemed as much a part of my daily environment as air.

In a few weeks, Conchita told us she and several other friends had finally come up with the money to rent another apartment.

"I'm happy for you, but I'll miss you," I said, giving her a hug. "I've learned so much Spanish just in the short time you've lived here—not to mention Catalan!"

"If you ever have that Bible study," she reminded me, "let me know, and I'll see if I can come. I'd still like to have that talk."

What a dear. A number of other friends from the residencia joined us for a good-bye supper for Conchita. We cooked it in our room on that lone burner. Then we all went out to a café for after-supper coffee and pastries. As they shared cigarettes and lights, I felt like I was missing out on part of the intimacy of friendship. I couldn't share in this passing of a modern day "peace" pipe.

I went shopping the next day and finally found a coat for 50 percent off.

"Wow!" Nancy whistled when I twirled around for her back at the residencia. "You look great! You look so . . . European."

"That Salvation Army special just didn't do much for me, did it?"

"Well, don't worry about it now," Nan said kindly. "And guess what. You can wear your new coat tonight.

We're all going out with Jim to an Italian restaurant, so he won't be so homesick."

"Do you really think he'll go home?"

"I don't know. He sure was down when I was talking to him today."

"It would be a shame to go home now."

"Oh I don't know. Why stick it out if you're miserable? Sometimes I just want to be with Mickey so bad."

Maybe Jim was right about the university. In the following week, three times my professors didn't show up for class at all. Was there a shutdown brewing?

On Saturday morning, we finally conducted the first of our Bible studies with two U.S. girls and two Spanish. We began by looking at Jesus and who he claimed to be. Bonnie also came for moral support, although Ruth had stressed that, in a study with non-Christians, it was wise not to overload the group with believers. That could make people feel outnumbered. It threw Cathy and me when the girls proceeded to smoke all the way through the study.

"I go to mass every weekend when I'm home," Concha commented, "but it doesn't mean much. The same old thing. We always had to make up some sin to share with the priest in confession."

"I remember in Catholic school the nuns would try to help us think of things to tell in confession," the girls said, giggling.

"I guess that's why I'm not practicing anymore," Deb threw in. "The church is dead. How can I know whether God exists?" Later Deb refused to be drawn in to the conversation at all, saying, "I'm just not interested."

I prayed Deb wouldn't turn me off, wouldn't write off me and our friendship. Maybe it would help if I didn't push. I didn't mention the Bible study when everyone else left, going on like nothing had happened. She was still my friend.

A heavy load of six classes kept my weeks more than full, but I had purposely taken extra classes in case I didn't make it in some of them.

The Friday after our first Bible study, Nancy told us there was another U.S. ship in port. She had met some fellows who were just new Christians. She thought it was important for us to spend the afternoon with several who wanted companionship—so they wouldn't be tempted by the more exotic pleasures available in Barcelona.

They were from the American South. It was so good to hear their accents, but not good to hear their prejudice.

"Those coloreds," said my "date," watching a black and white couple at a café near the Barcelona USO club. "They think they run the ship."

"Probably not any more than the whites," I probed, deciding I had little to lose by speaking my mind. But I had to remind myself they were new Christians. Given time and encouragement, Christ would bring growth.

"You lived in the North too long," he said, backing down.

We got out of the date about 5:30, because I had one class that met at the unthinkable hour of 7:00 p.m. on Fridays. That night, though, I couldn't bring myself to go, after an afternoon of goofing off.

"I guess it won't hurt to cut one class," I told Cathy, as we headed for a movie together.

I left next morning to spend the weekend with Concha at her home. She lived in the outlying city of Manresa, about an hour and a half by train from Barcelona.

No one was home when we arrived about noon. But she showed me through their one-floor, nicely decorated flat. In the foyer was a beautiful Persian rug, gold mirror, and entrance table. The dining room held another Persian rug, stately hutch, china cabinet, and table where they ate all meals. Then there was a small sitting area with a TV.

Concha's room was any girl's dream come true. It looked professionally decorated, although Concha claimed she had done it herself, even the wall papering. In addition to the sitting room, there was a large study-recreation room with piano, loads of books, and a sumptuous red velvet couch. Tasteful, original artwork including paintings by a son and the mother, lined the walls.

But when Concha showed me the kitchen, my mouth dropped. In a tiny room, two burners served as the stove. A dorm-sized refrigerator kept a few things cold. But there really wasn't need for a larger one since, like all Spanish women, her mother shopped every day for fresh vegetables, fruit, and meat.

After the grand tour, Concha drove us out to the country club to meet her friends. We watched several playing tennis, then Concha proudly introduced me as her "other American roommate." (Deb had visited Concha's hometown the weekend before.)

I felt out of my element, but not because of language. It was the first country club I'd ever been to in my life. Back at the "apartment," Concha introduced me to her brothers. The philosophy major gave me a weak handshake, then went back to his room to prepare for the students he tutored in Greek and Latin.

I had to think about the Spanish anthropology we had studied. Not too long ago in Catalonia, this oldest brother would have stood to inherit the total estate, with younger siblings getting nothing.

Thus the younger children in such families frequently left the family farm. They migrated to the cities in search of their fortune—or any livelihood at all. And so the cities in northern Spain tended to industrialize and grow more rapidly than in other parts of Spain.

Nowadays, though, it was the younger siblings who were considered lucky. They were *not* expected to stay home and farm, but were free to pursue careers as doctors, lawyers, or whatever.

The younger brother, Pedro Miguel, strode into the room at a commanding height (for a Spaniard), gave me a good, firm handshake and said, "So you're Melodie. Welcome."

"Thank you. I'm enjoying Manresa very much," I said, trying not to show what was really impressing me.

"But how do you like Spain? Is it really different from the United States?"

He poured out questions so fast I barely had time to answer one before he went to the next. He was in his fifth year of study to be a pediatrician. His crinkly eyes and friendly smile captivated me.

He's this friendly with every one, I told myself. It's his personality.

"How lovely this apartment is," I exclaimed.

102

The mother said, "Yes, but in the United States, you have so many appliances and things."

"And Melodie lives in a *house*—everyone lives in *separate* houses!" Concha bragged.

"Well, in the cities, they have apartments like this. Only not usually whole *floors*," I explained.

"But I think it would be so neat to have a separate house," continued Concha.

Finally, at 3:00 p.m., Señora Brugue was ready to serve dinner, which started with before-dinner martinis. Next came a course that was kind of a cream of wheat soup. It was followed by lettuce and olive salad, french-fried potatoes, then a lamb chop, washed down with carbonated water.

All these items were served on separate plates, as separate courses. For dessert Señora Brugue brought out classic Spanish flan (custard-like pudding), plus fruit. She topped all of it off with their best wine—the same stuff used in church communion services. After all this was cleared away, we finished with tiny demitasse cups of strong coffee.

An hour and a half of dining! I got the impression this would have been a more normal meal for Sunday than Saturday (Concha and I would be skiing on Sunday) and that touches like the communion wine were an extra treat for the guest.

I was overwhelmed. Once again I wished I could have lived with a family all year. It felt good to be in a home, to feel "fussed over."

"We simply must take you to our famous sacred mountains," Concha's mother said as we pushed away from the table.

"The mountains of Monserrat are shaped so differently—you'll love it." Concha explained as we got ready. "You have to go up by cable car."

I didn't have the heart to tell them I'd already been there with my own parents, so I was tickled to see Pedro Miguel getting into the car also.

At Monserrat, I oohed and aahed in the appropriate places like I'd never been there. I *was* impressed that it seemed a pilgrimage for Concha's mother, a place to get in touch again with the thirst for God that laps at everyone's heart. How different to see the monastery through the eyes of a faithful Catholic, rather than my parents' and my critical Protestant eyes.

We went to Saturday evening mass then, to justify skipping out on Sunday to go skiing in the mountains. After a 9:30 supper, Concha, Pedro Miguel, and I went to a movie.

By this time I knew Pedro's companionship was just that—making a guest feel at home. Again, how different from the men on the streets who made you feel at odds rather than welcome.

Concha's mother was waiting with snacks when we got home, wanting to ask me more about the United States. Suddenly I remembered all the students from abroad who had stayed at our house when I was young. We had kept them up to all hours talking, too, while they suffered through yawns.

It was difficult to get up at 6:30 the next morning, even for someone eager to ski for the first time. I had never gotten a chance to ski over Christmas. Concha was even more excited, like a girl heading for the beach.

104

"For me, skiing is like a drug," Concha exclaimed, as we packed poles and boots into the little car with four other people. "I gotta have it. It gives me a high that gets me through the week."

She apparently was quite good. I felt like I was in a commercial, zooming along the high mountain roads in Concha's friend's snazzy red sports car.

On the slopes I rode ski lifts and finally got up enough nerve to try a little skiing, using another girl's equipment. It was hard! How could Concha zoom down those hills? How, exactly, were you supposed to get up once you fell down?

On the way back the kids knew where to find a perfect little Catalan inn, tucked back in a small village. It was a meal I'll never forget, perfect in ambiance, camaraderie, and flavor of food.

First they brought us huge hunks of toasted bread with tomato and olive oil rubbed generously on the bread. The main course was sausage, ribs, and Catalan beans (something like white soup beans). I peeked in the kitchen and discovered an open fire where the meat had been prepared.

On a student budget, the bill of $40 for ten people was pure extravagance. Once again I felt like I was dreaming. Everyone was Catalan but me, and they soon gave up the considerable effort to remember to speak in Castillian. I was too wrapped up in the wonder of the evening to care.

I hit bottom fast when I went to my Monday evening class (the same one that met on Friday evening). I noticed a different mood in the class. Everyone was busily poring over notes, rather than smoking and waiting for the prof.

He came in on time. "Put away your books, and take out a clean paper," he said brusquely.

What is this? I groaned.

"Your exam will consist of this question—" and he rattled on about some obscure point of literary criticism. My face grew red.

"When did he announce this?" I hissed the best I could to a neighbor.

Friday. The day I'd cut. I took out a sheet of paper and wrote a long letter to Mom and Dad. I told them all about the wonderful weekend I'd had and about the class I was now flunking. I wrote for as long as the rest of the students wrote. Then I left without handing anything in. That was the end of that class. It was a relief. I felt like laughing and crying.

On Monday night, we had another Bible study. This time it was my turn to lead. I dared not fail, so I muddled my way through. Sometimes the discussion seemed to revolve only around the differences between Catholics and Protestants.

"We were just brought up different," Cynta, another new arrival at the residencia, concluded kindly. "You have your way, and we have ours."

I was thankful for my weekend of needing to talk Spanish so much—it helped my fluency in the Bible study. But next time I would simply have to prepare better.

"I'm actually beginning to think in Spanish sometimes," I marveled to Nancy.

"I know—it really helps to have Spanish roommates," Nancy agreed. "Remember how disappointed we all were at the beginning of the year when we had to come to the residencia?" I nodded.

"Now I think we're the lucky ones. We have an easy way to have friendships with Spanish girls our own age. All the other kids living in families have to make a special effort to find Spanish friends."

Nancy was probably right. Although I enjoyed my Cinderella weekend in Concha's home, it might have gotten tiring to be fussed over all the time. Indeed, I knew from other students that lack of privacy and continual urgings to "eat, eat, eat" had become a real problem.

Even at the residencia the Spanish penchant for companionship sometimes got to me. The girls there seemed to rarely do anything alone; they frequently came to our room for coffee or to talk. Anything, it seemed, to keep me from studying.

To escape, sometimes I'd go to one of Barcelona's cheap cafés and sit for hours. A cup of coffee was the only ticket one needed; the waiters never hurried you out or gave menacing looks. I'd read, study, write, or just think. When I ran out of money for coffee, I'd sneak into the always-open doors of the various cathedrals around town.

No matter what time of day you went into a church, at least a half dozen or so women (sometimes men) would be scattered on various pews throughout the sanctuary. They prayed the rosary and gazed silently at a gaudy crucifix often decorated with plastic flowers.

The thick stone walls of the cathedral were always cold and damp, bringing little warmth on days when Barcelona cold stuck in your bones like a bad ache. But sitting next to a shawled, black-garbed woman, her fanning hips nudging mine, a certain warmth flowed from her body to mine.

Isn't that always the way it is in church? I reflected. The building offers no warmth or refuge in itself—but the presence of other human beings does!

The Campus Crusade associates in Spain often reminded us that the majority of people in Spain could be considered pagan, but in my heart I could not consider these dear women that. Here they were, seeking God, caught up in some spiritual mystery like Concha's mother, meditating on the ultimate sacrifice of Jesus Christ. I knew that many of these women came to the church on a daily basis, praying faithfully more hours a day than I ever managed.

Maybe there were things I could learn about being a Christian from my Catholic friends.

12

Out of the Salt Shaker

My care package finally arrived in February, after more than four months enroute.

"The stuff will probably be moldy," warned Nancy.

Mom had taped it like it was going to the moon, so when we finally got it open I shrieked, "Pecans!"

Concha grabbed the two-pound bag from our Florida pecan grove and matched my pitch.

"Do you know how much these are worth?"

"I have no idea. A couple dollars in the States."

"Here they are worth—oh, I don't know either, but I know they're too expensive ever to have a bag that big."

What fun, to open this box now with a Spanish friend. "Cookies!" she exclaimed. "Did your mother *make* these?"

"Yes."

"I just can't understand how you know how to make cookies and cakes and things. We always get them from the bakery."

"Cookies are usually what small children learn to bake first!"

There was a Kraft macaroni dinner, popcorn, boxes of instant soup, and the few things I had requested earlier. And last, there was a brand-new Bible—my Christmas present close to Valentine's Day!

On Valentine's Day, Deb wanted me to go with her on a blind date. She had met a guy with Tara's roommate, Cynta, at the Trocadero discotheque. And this guy had a "friend."

"Aw, come on, Deb. A blind date?"

"It will be good Spanish practice. Besides, it's Valentine's Day."

"Huh, they never heard of Valentine's Day here. What about Larry? What would he say?"

"We're both free to date others while I'm over here. He agrees to that. As long as it's nothing serious."

"Oh well, why not?" I finally agreed.

My date looked as skeptical as I about this blind date. Deb's friend introduced us both and said, "Melodie, this is Casi Miro—he almost sees you," then laughed broadly.

I smiled weakly, knowing just enough Spanish to slowly catch the play on words. *Casi Miro* means "almost saw." I also felt weak because he was the best-looking guy I'd ever been out with. What would he think of me?

"Doesn't he look just like Mark Spitz, the swimmer?" Deb's date was saying.

I nodded, finally realizing why my *head* was swimming. He *was* a dead ringer for Spitz.

We walked to a neighborhood restaurant and chatted politely. "Deb says you're with a band," I began.

"Yes, I studied engineering. But for the last two

110

years I've been doing what I really love—writing lyrics for our band."

"That's neat!" I exclaimed. "I do some writing myself."

For the first time, Casi Miro looked like he *was* finally seeing me. "Oh, really! That's very interesting. Maybe we have something in common."

I swallowed. He smiled. "What do you write?"

"A little bit of everything. I write for our school paper at home. Poetry. I've written some articles for a youth magazine."

"Well, a real writer!" Casi Miro reached for my hand. I kept telling myself not to get excited. Such a good-looking guy couldn't possibly stay interested long. Or else he only wanted one thing.

"Let's take them to that bar over on Paseo de Gracia," Casi Miro told his friend, hailing a taxi.

It turned out to be a posh, expensive place with waiters scurrying to light women's cigarettes and deep, secluded booths for intimate conversation. I felt once again like I was Cinderella, wondering when the clock would strike and my prince would be gone.

We continued to talk, Casi Miro correcting my Spanish all the while. "I have an *obsession* for Castilian," he explained, being from Madrid and living in Barcelona. "I can't stand to hear how everyone butchers Castilian in this city!"

"You must have a hard time hearing my Spanish, then," I lamented.

"I can help you. I'll help you talk better Spanish," Casi Miro said soothingly, ending with a kiss.

I sighed happily. "You know, that's the first time I've been kissed in over a year."

"Really? That's interesting. Because that's the first time I've kissed a girl in over two years!"

I didn't believe him. A Spanish guy as good-looking as he not involved with any women? What did he take me for?

"Pepe," Casi Miro called to his friend on the other side of the booth. "Tell Melodia here that I haven't had any girlfriends for two years."

"Yes, it's true. We've been so busy with the band. No time for girls."

I looked at Deb. We rolled our eyes.

"They don't believe us!" Pepe exclaimed. "Now me, I've made time for girls. But Casi Miro here, it's the truth."

He kissed me again.

"So now you are trying to make up for lost time?" I joked. He laughed.

"We must go home," I said to Deb a few minutes later.

"Yes, we really have to go," she nodded.

"But we were going to take you to where the band practices. Show you our instruments."

"You'll have to do that another time. The residencia gets locked at midnight," I said firmly.

"Yes, yes, another time," Pepe finally agreed.

Deb knew I was reeling from the events of the evening. "And you didn't want to go on a blind date," she mocked.

I couldn't stop smiling. "He really did look like Mark Spitz, didn't he?"

"Yes, he really did."

"Pepe was good looking too."

"That's okay; you don't have to try to make me feel better. You did this as a favor to me, remember. And don't worry. Larry is still the number one man in my life," Deb finished.

I left Deb sleeping in on Sunday morning (Concha had gone home for the weekend, as usual,) to catch the bus to church with Cathy.

"Big night last night?" she said, smiling.

"Yeah!" I replied, launching into most if not all the details.

"I'm glad you had a chance to go out."

She said it genuinely, though I knew she thought I was playing with fire in going out with a guy who wasn't a Christian. I knew, too, how badly she wanted a special relationship with a guy.

Pastor Martinez had a wonderful sermon that morning about how Christians had to be the salt of the earth. Salt is a preservative. Christians must cling to their morals and beliefs in a world of decay. This means knowing what you believe and why, he said. But he didn't stop there, reminding us that salt doesn't do any good in the salt shaker. Christians can't do any good clumped in nice, little fellowships, he said, but have to do their preserving out in the world.

Was my going out with Deb and her friends a good example of "salt out of the saltshaker"? Or had I crossed over the line and lost any saltiness? Was I simply going along with everything and everyone around me? The old question—how to live *in* but not be part of the world still haunted me.

We had requested prayer from people back home for the Monday night Bible study. It met at 10:00. This was a good time for us, because it came right after the Spanish girls had finished their supper but before we were ready to wind down for the night.

But this Monday, the late nights of the weekend showed in the yawns and restlessness of a couple of the girls. We plainly weren't getting anywhere, at least that we could tell.

"I just wish they wouldn't have to *smoke* during the Bible study!" Cathy gritted her teeth as we talked privately the next day. "I think it's really rude—drives me up the wall."

"But it makes them feel like it's their turf, makes them feel more at home," I pointed out. Maybe our thinking of the group in terms of "us" and "them" was part of the problem.

"Well, we knew we weren't really equipped to lead a study like this in Spanish," I added. "If God wants to accomplish anything, it will have to be in spite of us—it's God's study."

"That's true," Cathy agreed.

That week I prepared for the Monday night study like it was a final exam, writing out the complete text of what I wanted to say in Spanish. It was from John 8, where Jesus finally confronts the leaders who opposed him in an open debate. The Pharisees were saying that Jesus couldn't witness on his own behalf, implying that he was lying about himself.

"There are basically four ways we can look at the claims of Jesus," I told the girls in the study, repeating ideas I'd heard from someone else. "One, that Jesus was a liar of tremendous proportions; two, that he was completely crazy; three, that it was all just a legend; or four, that Jesus was telling the truth about himself when he said he was the Son of God, light of the world.

"If Jesus was trying to deceive the people, in our studies so far we haven't seen the personality traits of one who is trying to deceive. So, do you think Jesus really was God?"

They looked a little glazed. Maybe it was because, in spite of my best preparation, the truths of John 8 were theologically heavy in one's own language, let alone interpreted by a foreigner. Maybe it was the smoke or the hour. Or maybe something really was getting through.

The next week the strike we had been hearing rumors about finally happened. Half of my profs didn't show up for class. How grateful I was for dear Mrs. Burns and her English literature class. As a citizen of Britain, she also watched the university system with the amused detachment of an outsider and conducted her classes like clockwork. I would have at least one solid class on my credits.

The strikes should have meant more time for study but we lost time waiting around the university to see which classes would meet. In theory, the strike was for more pay. Beyond that, Barcelona had been a seedbed of university protest against iron rule from Madrid, ever since the first demonstrations had erupted there in 1968.

Of course, as some of the residenica girls said, the pay was poor because the teachers weren't any good. With no set educational requirements for teachers, quality was difficult to maintain. It was a vicious cycle.

I was glad for the weekend and another date with Casi Miro. But he and Pepe called to cancel at the last minute.

"No girls in two years—ha!" I laughed. "How naive does he think I am, anyway? He must have found something better for tonight."

"We really did have a conflict," Casi Miro explained when we met them the next night. "Had to see about an engagement for the band."

"Maybe they'll believe we have a band if we take them to see where we practice," Pepe added.

We wound through back streets till we came to a locked, grille-covered door. Pepe unlocked it. Inside, as promised, were the instruments and several rooms separated by windows and soundproofing material.

"Turn on the stereo," Casi Miro called to Pepe. Then the two of us went to a room separate from Deb and Pepe.

"So this is where you practice?" I said, trying to keep the conversation going.

"Yes, almost every night. It gets really loud in here," he laughed.

It was chilly in the unheated basement. I shivered. Casi Miro put his arm around me.

"It was so good to kiss you the other night," Casi Miro said, breathing heavily. He pulled me to the padded floor of the vocal booth. "I just had to have more."

"So this is why you brought us here," I muttered. Some date.

"No, no, but now that we're here—" he said softly.

"Wait a minute. Kissing you is one thing," I said, grasping not only for the proper Spanish. "Let's just stick to that."

"Why? We're alone. I'm a man, you're a woman." He may have been smooth with his lines in the beginning, but now he was beginning to sound like just another guy with a lot of lines.

I struggled to get up. He pulled me back down. "Wait, let Deb and Pepe have their privacy," he cautioned.

I sat on the floor. I couldn't hear anything coming from the other room. But then, these were soundproof rooms. Surely Deb wouldn't—yet she had told me she took birth control pills. Or what if he forced her? Maybe I was lucky Casi Miro was enough of a gentleman to stop.

I tried to think of something to say. Casi Miro was so good-looking. "You know, I really like you, but this is all moving a little fast."

"Yeah, okay. So I got carried away."

"What are we supposed to do? Just wait for them?"

The door opened. Deb emerged, looking a little disheveled but okay.

Pepe spoke to Casi Miro. "She wants to go."

"Yeah, us too," Casi Miro said. We found a convenient way to end the evening and hurry home.

"So how'd your date go?" I asked Deb. She looked at me as if I'd just been born. "They had it planned all along, didn't they?"

Deb shook her head. "I don't know. *Who* knows? Are you all right?"

"Yeah, sure, I'm fine."

"He just couldn't understand why I wouldn't make love to him. I tried to tell him we were just friends, and that for me there was a big step between sleeping with

117

a friend and sleeping with someone you were in love with. I just kept telling him that over and over, and finally I guess he believed I wasn't going to do it."

Silently I cheered. So Deb had her standards, even though they weren't quite the same as mine.

"I don't think Casi Miro will ask me out again," I sighed, a little regretfully.

"You won't be missing much," Deb said, shrugging.

"But he was so cute!"

"Mel! Oh, I know, I know. He was definitely good-looking. It was good experience, wasn't it?"

I laughed. "Yeah, I never tried to talk such perfect Spanish in my life, not even for my professors!"

"He really had a thing about it, didn't he?"

What a friend. We walked the last block to the residencia in comfortable silence.

The contents of my care package didn't last long. It seemed as if Spanish girls were looser with possessions than I was used to.

"Hope you don't mind that I borrowed some of your cookies," Cynta said one day.

"Sure, help yourself," I said, minding very much. Why did I have to be that way, counting every cracker as if I were a miser?

"Mel, can I use some of your Trinaranjos juice for supper?" Concha asked.

Why didn't she buy her own? She was obviously wealthier than I was.

"Go right ahead," I smiled.

Sharing cigarettes, clothes, food. What's mine is yours was the prevailing philosophy. Quite biblical, really. But I resented it.

One Saturday afternoon, I just had to get away. I fled to a woods not far from the residencia that I had discovered a few months earlier. It was my thinking place, my place to be alone, a place to write in my journal.

"We spend so much time in the room just talking, chatting, laughing," I penned (now in Spanish) in my journal. I wrote in Spanish for the practice but also because certain expressions came easier. "I think I must be selfish—I don't like sharing all my things. I guess the last straw was when someone broke my cassette player."

A week later, I'd swung to the opposite pendulum. I wrote, "Time is passing so fast. And we're having so much fun! Tonight five of us from the residencia went out for pizza with everything on it. Then, walking home, we found a small park. We played on the teeter-totters, the slides, the swings. How good to be children again for a few moments!

"I'm so happy to be finally *talking* Spanish. Oh, sure, I make lots of mistakes. But at least I'm making mistakes, and not sitting there with my mouth closed like an idiot. I feel so sorry for Cindy, Nola, and others who don't really have much opportunity to talk Spanish.

"Now all that I lack is a boyfriend. I don't think Casi Miro will call again, not that I should go out with him. Everyone at home expects me to come home with a Spanish boyfriend. Ha!" my journal entry closed.

Late at night, I'd light candles and listen to tapes of Joan Baez or James Taylor and pinch myself. Someday, I told myself, you'll be old and married and longing for the days when you were single and wishing a special someone would call you on the phone.

One Sunday, early in March, I woke up with a sick headache. I felt like throwing up. I took some pills with my morning coffee, went back to bed, and woke two hours later feeling much better.

Nancy hadn't gone to church either. We decided to go to Plaza Cataluña to get pictures of toddlers feeding pigeons there like they always did, especially on Sundays.

"I've really got to get some of these things on camera," I told Nancy. "I can't believe we only have about four months left in Spain."

"I know. I'm so torn. I really love it here, yet I want to be with Mickey so bad." She looked so lonesome in that instant that I thought maybe it was better *not* to have a boyfriend back home.

"Let's go down to the cathedral. Maybe we can get some pictures of the *sardana* dancers there."

"Yeah, they're usually dancing Sunday noon," Nan said eagerly.

As we neared my favorite section of the city, we could hear chanting. There were lots of people milling around. "Must be the sardana dancers," I told Nancy.

But as we got closer, we couldn't see any dancers. There were about 150 students sitting on the steps of the cathedral. They were chanting about Puig, a political criminal who had been executed the day before in the prison near the cathedral. Rumor was that the execution was performed by a wire tightened slowly around his neck.

The demonstrators were shouting, "Franco is a dictator!" and "Franco, the assassin." After a while they got up and started walking toward another street, still chanting. One fellow covered his face with his coat as he passed us. I wasn't sure what we had walked into, but I decided I was going to get a picture of it.

"No, no, no!" Another guy came and put his hand in front of the camera. *"Don't take our picture."*

I quickly dropped my camera. In my naïveté, I hadn't thought about what photographing demonstrators could mean.

"Ooohgha, ooohgha." We heard the unforgettable sound of European police wagons racing through the narrow streets. Everyone started to run. We did too. Hiding behind a column, I snapped a picture of one of the *grises* (gray-clad police), then made sure my camera was safely in my shoulder bag.

When we returned to the residencia that evening, the girls were abuzz with rumors about the university. Would it be open? Would there be trouble if we went, identifying ourselves with the students? What real danger could anyone be in, really, if they didn't do anything? I wondered how much of the talk was Spanish hyperbole.

"But why are they so upset about Puig?" I asked.

"Capital punishment is so barbaric for one thing," Cynta shrieked, just like she always did when excited. "There hasn't been anyone executed for a political crime in ten years. It shows how bad things are getting again. Modern societies are getting *rid* of capital punishment, not bringing it back!"

Puig had become a symbol of all the students felt was wrong with Spain—the general repression of freedom of expression, the central control from Madrid over regions that had their own languages, culture, history.

At the university on Monday, black flags hung around the patio. Posters proclaimed, "Let it be the last crime of the regime" and "The dictator is an assassin."

I decided to go to my classes. Surprisingly, Professor Marcos showed up. He launched into his usual "commentary on a text," droning on and on.

Suddenly a loud cry went up on the patio. "Grises!"

Marco stopped. We all stiffened. Another cry, then two students entered the classroom, telling us all to leave in solidarity with the protest. We quickly gathered our things and left through the small door in the wall surrounding the university. We saw busloads of police outside the university door.

Caman arranged for an informal gathering of students who were worried about their studies during the time of unrest. "Just make sure you carry your passport all the time, and if anyone arrests you, tell them you're a U.S. citizen. They'll let you go fast because they don't want bad publicity," he advised.

"Is it really dangerous? You hear so many rumors," Lucille asked.

"No, I don't think so. As long as you don't do something really stupid, you'll be fine."

Finally the university officially closed down for a long weekend, probably to calm things down. On the Thursday night it closed, students gathered for a memorial service honoring Puig in the big cathedral close to where he had been executed. The cathedral was filled with students. Afterward, they left in total silence and walked all the way up the Ramblas.

"You should have seen it," Concha reported proudly. "This has earned the students a lot of respect. It was really something! And the police didn't make us disperse!"

Classes resumed peacefully the next week. But I knew we had been through something important with our new friends.

More and more each remaining day of my time in Spain became a gift to savor. With warmer days in March, I found frequent excuses to hide away in my woods retreat. Sometimes I took along a thick Spanish sandwich of freshly made bread, a delicate cheese, and tomato rubbed in the bread. What fun it would be, I thought, to be sharing this picnic with a guy.

Why did dreams of romance always edge in on perfect moments, whittling away at my contentment? Why had all the men I'd met this year turned out to be little more than one-time dates? Was there something wrong with me? Or was I hearing a still, small voice nudging me toward being single for life?

"The possibility of my remaining single keeps running through my mind," I bravely wrote home to my parents. "I don't want you to claim me as a dependent next year on your income tax." If I was going to be single, I might as well start planning for my independence and make the most of it.

13

Where Do I Stand?

All of a sudden, spring spread over Barcelona. My first surprise was that the Spanish university girls at the residencia liked to "lay out" as much as their U.S. counterparts. We headed to the roof of the residencia and, while the maid hung out our bedsheets up there, we lounged and rotisseried ourselves in the brilliant Mediterranean sun.

"Let's go to the beach this weekend," I suggested. "I've been wanting to go to down to Sitges all year—and this is a long weekend coming up, with the holiday on Monday."

"I don't think I can afford it," Cathy sighed.

Nancy added, "I've got too many papers to work on."

"I think I'll go myself and stay overnight. Why don't you two join me on Saturday?" I persisted.

"I could go for that," Cathy consented.

"I guess I could go that long. Work on our tans," said Nancy.

Concha couldn't believe we'd go to the beach so

early. She was still skiing on weekends in the mountains.

"We'll probably look like the tourists who come down to Florida and try to swim in December," I laughed. "But who cares? We *are* tourists."

Eagerly I set out by myself on Friday after school. I took the train to the coastal village of Sitges, about an hour's ride. In March the town was deserted, but all the more scenic for lack of crowds. The sun shone on the whitewashed town, making it stand out against the blue sky. It looked just like the postcards sold in Sitges's many souvenir stores.

After finding a nice, clean hotel room for $2 a night, I walked one block to the beach. The crash of ocean waves swept me up in a rush of homesickness for Florida, mixed with a fierce love for this new land of mine. Did anything compare to walking barefoot in the sand, hearing the surf, feeling the spring sun on your face, glancing at a picture-perfect village on land?

Truth be told, I *was* once again wary about being all by myself as a female in a strange town. Yet I was exhilarated to navigate in Spanish, on my own. As the sun set, I walked fast and purposefully, like they tell you to do to ward off unwanted advances.

"A table for one?" The maître d' at the hotel looked at me with a raised eyebrow.

I suppose it was a little unusual—a young woman by herself at a hotel on a Friday night.

"Yes," I told him confidently, trying to act elegant, not cheap. A table for *one*. If I was to remain single, I would have to get used to the sound.

I ordered a complete four-course meal of soup, omelet, and pork chops in a savory sauce. I was enjoying my dessert of flan when I noticed another table for one. The man was watching me, a little amused. His haircut had "Army" written all over it.

As I left the dining room, planning to spend the rest of the night in my room, "Army" walked up. He said, "I couldn't help noticing you walking on the beach this afternoon. I thought to myself, There goes a girl born in the USA."

My face turned crimson. He'd gotten the reaction he wanted.

"How could you know?"

"Spanish girls don't walk like you were walking."

"What do you mean?"

"Oh, you know, like they were ready to take on the whole world, or as if to say 'better not try to mug me, man.'"

I had to laugh. "So my country of origin was sticking out all over?"

He grinned in return. "Are you . . . alone?"

"Well, yes, if it's any of your business. I'm enjoying a night by myself. Two friends are joining me here tomorrow."

"I'm lonely," Army admitted. "You wouldn't consider keeping a poor soldier company tonight, would you?"

He seemed perceptive even if not very good-looking. Should I let myself be picked up? I was sure I'd have little in common with him, but at least I wouldn't be stuck in my room the rest of the night. "What's your name?"

"Harlan. Yours?"

"Melodie."

"How pretty. Just like you."

"Thank you, but if I keep you company, you have to understand it's only that. I . . . I'm not interested in a date."

"That's how women usually are with me," Harlan sighed. "Sure, sure, no commitments. I'll keep my hands off you," he promised, raising his hands.

I laughed.

"You sure are pretty when you smile. You should do it more often. You looked so serious out there on the beach."

"How long did you watch me?

"All afternoon."

"Aw, come on. Why didn't I see you?"

"Military training."

"It makes me feel funny—vulnerable. Like what crackpot could be watching me and I wouldn't even know it."

"That's another reason I thought I should keep you company tonight."

"I wasn't going to go out. I was just going to my room. Besides, I wouldn't know where to go in this village."

"That's why you need me. There's a little English bar a couple streets over that has games—darts and a pinball machine."

"English?"

"Yeah, for all the tourists from Europe and England who come down."

"What are you doing here, anyway?"

"Just a little R and R."

"Where are you stationed?"

"Oh, southern Germany," he said vaguely. "A lot of guys come down here for vacation."

"Are you alone?"

"Nah. I came with another guy who has a car over here. He's got a date tonight."

"A car over here?"

"Yeah, a great big boat, especially compared to these foreign jobs. Wait till you see it."

I don't plan to know you that long, I said to myself, but there was something about Harlan that saddened me. He did seem really lonely, and he had come here with a friend. Here I had been alone but not at all lonely.

He bought me a drink later. We walked the beach some more, till finally I insisted I wanted to go to my room.

"Okay. See, I kept my hands off, didn't I?"

"Yes. I enjoyed the evening. Good night."

It seemed like a week had passed when Nancy and Cathy finally joined me the next morning. We changed in my room and hit the beach, only to be joined shortly by Harlan and his friend, Matt.

Matt plopped down on the blanket beside Nancy, already taken by her blond good looks, to say nothing of her swim suit. Harlan stood awkwardly beside Cathy, and finally I took the hint to introduce them all.

"This is the guy who could tell I was from the States just by the way I walked!" I made a face, and they all laughed.

"This is Cathy, from Pennsylvania, and this is Nancy, who's practically engaged to a West Point officer," I said pointedly for the benefit of Matt.

128

"Oooh. West Point." You could tell by the way he said it that it only made the challenge that much bigger. He had a brown paper bag under his arm, molded in the shape of a bottle.

With Nancy in the crowd, it didn't take the conversation long to turn to spiritual matters—really! Harlan was soon telling us how he had given up on the church long ago, and Matt didn't have any interest.

"But how can you live just for your next R and R?" Nancy continued. "Life has to be more than just the next weekend. Believe me, I know."

"I can't believe my luck!" Harlan exclaimed. "One of the reasons I wanted to come down here was to get away from some buddies on the base who've been bugging me about God!" Harlan muttered.

"Really?" Cathy asked.

"And what do I do but run into a nice girl and her two friends, and all they want to talk about is God."

Cathy couldn't resist the lead-in. "You don't think someone's trying to say something to you, do you?"

"Well I don't know. I've made such a mess of my life—"

I lay back down on the blanket, glad Cathy seemed interested in really talking with Harlan. As usual, her ability to care for anyone, no matter what they looked like, impressed me. Nancy, on the other side of me, was pressing Matt about his spiritual disinterest as well. Finally everyone was famished.

"Let's go get some cheese and fruit and stuff and have a little picnic," Nancy suggested.

We walked down to a pier of rocks jutting out into the ocean, where waves crashed up on the rocks.

Shouting to hear each other, we shared bread and wine out there as if in a magazine ad.

The picture was spoiled only by Matt's drinking too much, maybe because of his failure to conquer Nancy—or forget her preaching.

It was time to get back to Barcelona. "Don't bother to take the train. We'll take you in the car," said Matt.

"Nah, we'll just take the train," I said, wanting to get away from Matt now.

"Don't be silly. We have to go that way anyway. I insist," said Matt. Harlan shrugged his shoulders.

Matt left to get the car, and we gathered up our things. As we headed up the curving, oceanfront road toward Barcelona, it soon became obvious that Matt must have grabbed another drink when he went to get the car.

"Better let Harlan drive," Nancy said to Matt.

"Nonsense. I can drive perfectly well," Matt replied, slurring the words. He careened over the center line, then pulled back as a car came from the other direction. For the first time in my life, I knew the terror of being in a vehicle with a drunk driver.

"Stop or you'll kill us all," Harlan yelled to his friend. But Matt had turned vicious as well, cursing that he wasn't drunk. I could see the headlines back home: "U.S. students killed when soldier's car goes over cliff." If all year I had been telling myself a little drinking was harmless, this was a siren screaming about how dangerous it could become.

Cathy and I held hands and prayed in the back seat. We rounded another treacherous curve and came perilously near the edge.

Finally Nancy put her hand on Matt's arm, shame-lessly turning on the charm. "Please, please stop, for *me*. Let Harlan drive." She was almost in tears.

Matt jerked the car into a scenic overlook. He got out, swaggered around the back of the car, still cursing. Harlan quickly took over. Cathy and I breathed deep-ly, thankful this time for Nancy's way with guys. It might have just saved our lives.

No one talked the rest of the way to Barcelona. Matt mercifully went to sleep. Flashbacks of those cliff-hanging curves kept replaying in my mind.

"Thanks for being my friend," Harlan told Cathy, as we all said goodbye before catching the Metro at Plaza Cataluña. "Let me take you all out for lunch on Wednesday before I head back to Germany. You pick whatever place you want."

We looked at each other. "Can't turn that down!" Cathy smiled.

"Are you sure you can afford to take *all* of us?" I asked.

"I don't have anyone else to spend my money on," he replied. "You've really made me think about some things I didn't want to think about."

On the Metro home we had time to talk about the fact that all our Bible studies seemed to be ending with everyone just agreeing that we all had our own opin-ions about the Bible.

"Maybe it's time to call it off," I suggested. "I think we've done what we could, meeting for almost eight weeks now."

"I hate to disappoint the people back home who are praying for us," Cathy replied.

"I know. I *really* felt like a missionary when your mother's Bible study sent us that money for literature for our group!"

"That was so sweet," Nancy chimed in. "But maybe Mel is right. I think the study has done us as much good as anyone. It has forced us to prepare in a way we never would have if we hadn't had to present it to the group."

"That's really true," I added. "You know, just the other day, Tonia and I were talking, and we got into some things I never could have expressed in Spanish if I hadn't prepared that one study for the group."

"I just can't help feeling we're letting God down," Nancy sighed.

Maybe God is bigger than our puny efforts, I thought. Maybe God would continue to speak to our friends, just as we had been able to nurture the seeds planted in Harlan by his buddies in Germany.

By now I had gotten more used to the idea of there being genuine Christians in the military. Perhaps they were at a different place in their Christian walk than I, but who can possibly question the ways of God—always higher than our ways.

"So have you decided yet where you're going on spring vacation?" Cathy asked.

"I think I'll try London. A group of students from my college at home are there right now for a semester of study. And I just learned the other day that Anita from our group wants to go to England."

"That sounds wonderful."

"Have you decided where *you're* going, Cathy?"

"I think I'll see more of Spain, probably go south."

"It should be wonderfully warm."

Anita was one of the few students from a Brethren college. When I had gotten to know her a bit, I had been fascinated to learn that her major was peace studies. So many Brethren Colleges Abroad students didn't claim any faith. So it surprised me to learn that she took seriously, not only her faith, but also her Anabaptist understandings.

It felt odd that, while usually I would have identified more with her camp while at college in the U.S., here I had been plugged into an evangelical camp. From looks and whispers, I knew that some in our BCA group thought that Nancy, Cathy, Bonnie, and I, and one fellow were too good to mix with everyone else. Why else would we go off for coffee together after classes? But maybe others in the group were just as Christian as Anita. They just didn't want to identify with anything "holier than thou."

Where did I stand, anyway? Was it possible to somehow bridge the two groups? Was it, perhaps, imperative for Christians to work to find ways to bring together a fervor for witnessing *and* good works?

14

Springtime

Barcelona in spring was like spring everywhere. It was fresh and alive and bursting with thoughts that young folks turn to and all of that. We were already in pajamas one night when we heard the distinct sound of a banjo strumming near our windows.

"It's a serenade!" I cried, going off to get some of the other girls. "We're being serenaded!"

Looking out, we could make out five or six fellows with robes tied around their necks. They looked like troubadours from the sixteenth century.

"La tuna!" Concha yelled, explaining that the outfits were typically worn by traditional singing groups. From upstairs we heard the laughter of several of the Spanish residents. The banter and calls back and forth told us that the "tuna" had come for the girls upstairs, not us.

No matter. I grabbed my cassette player and caught a few snatches of the lilting ballad and chorus. The smell of new foliage and flowers rolled in with the song through the open window.

On Friday, I could barely force myself to go indoors for classes at the university. I was definitely up for something that night, but what? A feeling that I was going to meet someone special flashed through my mind. But it was the kind of premonition you only pay attention to after it has come true.

"Guess who we met coming home on the subway this noon," Cathy teased at our midday meal.

"Who?"

Cathy was enjoying the attention. "There are a bunch of U.S. guys who go to school right up here near the residencia at San Gervasio!"

"Really?" I asked. "I wonder why we haven't run into them before now?"

"I know, it's kinda strange. But they're a little young, I might as well warn you. They all go to a fancy prep school near Boston and are studying here this year," Nancy continued. "They asked us to go with them to a jazz concert tonight."

It wasn't fair. Two boyfriends in the States, and more offers than she could handle here.

"What about Mickey?"

"Oh, goodness, it's not a date. There are four of them."

"Do you think they'd mind if I came too? I kind of feel like going out."

"Sure, the more the merrier."

"And they're really young enough to be our kid brothers," Cathy repeated.

"I never went to a jazz concert before," I said, as we headed toward rendezvous point, Plaza Cataluña. "I can just hear my Mom: 'That noise isn't music!'"

"There they are," Cathy pointed, motioning to three clean-cut young guys waiting near the center of the plaza.

"This is our friend Melodie," Cathy said. "Hope you don't mind if she comes along."

"Don't mind at all," said the tallest one, looking me over and shaking my hand with a firm, friendly grip. "I'm Tobe, from New York."

"I'm Melodie. I've only been to New York once in my life, right before coming over here. And I've never been to a jazz concert," I gushed with uncharacteristic talkativeness.

"Well, you're in luck tonight," Tobe smiled, tucking my hand through his arm, the better to stroll along Spanish-style. "You just happen to be with a big fan of jazz. Big fan."

"How old are you, anyway?" I asked as we headed toward the theater.

"Twenty, almost twenty-one," he replied.

I thought he flushed just a little. Heads turned as we walked, but it certainly wasn't because of me. "Do you feel people looking at you?" I whispered.

"Yeah, it gets embarrassing. Little kids stare at me all the time. Old ladies come up and want to shake my hand."

Among the pale-skinned people of Barcelona, he definitely stood out, to say nothing of being probably a foot taller than the average Spanish man. I was fascinated, already under the spell of that charisma which a few people seem to be born with.

Through Tobe's eyes, I learned that jazz was best thought of as one instrument talking to another. "Do wop e do wop, ta ta ta," Tobe chanted with the music. "This is the only music that is truly native to the U.S.," he said.

He beat imaginary drums with his hands. "What I like about it is that it's always original, always comes out different." For the first time I really heard jazz as music, not noise.

Tobe held open doors, let others pass first. He was quite big but was tender as a child as he knelt down to talk with a little kid who was eying him. "I love little kids," he said as he stood up again. "Of course, the kids where I live get to be awful pests. I can hardly study."

"So you live with a family?"

"A wonderful family. The mother, she's just like Ma. Cooks wonderful meals. They have two kids who just love me. You'll love them. You just have to meet my family."

"Sure. I love to get into real Spanish homes," I replied, wondering if his inviting me "home" meant anything special. He *was* a little young for me, but so what?

After the concert, Tobe wanted us all to go to his favorite hangout, a discotheque near the port.

"Why not? It's Friday night. I could go for some dancing." Nancy's eyes sparkled.

But Tobe said "Oh, oh," as soon as we entered. "I have to go talk to someone."

I hung out with Cathy and Nancy and tried not to notice as he cornered a girl on the dance floor. Something crazy and jealous surged in me as I watched the girl dance slowly with Tobe. He was talking to her, then she pulled away and headed for the bathroom. Tobe walked back to me.

"Sorry about that," Tobe looked genuinely sad. "I've been going out with her but trying to break up. She was just so possessive. I never thought we'd run into her here."

"You mean you broke up with her, just like that?" I asked.

"Well, I told her I'd talk to her later, but that I really wanted to be with others and was with my friends tonight."

I swallowed, storing the information for future reference. But I soon forgot the girl as I danced with Tobe myself. So many temporary acquaintances all year. So many outings with fellows I didn't really care about. Wanting so desperately to have a special relationship with a guy. Now was this the beginning of something more lasting?

I had to laugh at my earlier letter, where I said, "I think I'm prepared to remain single for a long time." Or maybe it was *because* I had finally given up looking for a guy that Tobe came along.

I wanted the night to last forever, but Cathy told the guys, "We'll have to crawl in the windows at the residencia if we don't go soon." Then she caught my frown.

"Why don't you see if Tobe wants to come to church with us Sunday?" she said helpfully. As usual, Cathy was reading me with breath-catching accuracy.

"Church? Sure I'll go to church," Tobe returned. "If I can get out of bed."

When we were out of earshot, I asked Tobe, "Do you usually go to church? I mean, are you a Christian?" The question had been in the back of my mind

all evening. No use feeling serious things about someone who wasn't a Christian, I'd learned long ago.

"Yes, yes, I'm a Christian—in my own way."

I wondered what that meant. But for now his reply
was enough to send me to bed with a soothed con-
science. And a swimming head.

I awoke with Tobe on my mind, but now in the clear
light of Saturday morning. I stumbled to the dining
room of the residencia, enjoying the wonderful smell
of coffee coming up the shaft of the dumb waiter.

"Come in, come in," Deb invited. "Big date last
night, Mel?"

"Oh," I started. "Was I on another planet?"

Deb laughed. "I'd say he must be pretty special."

Tara watched me with an amused smile.

"The funny thing is, it really wasn't a date or anything. I just ended up with this big guy named Tobe."

"That's always the best way," Tara commented.

I smiled weakly. "Yeah, but it's doing things to my
concentration. And I have so much studying to do before we go on spring vacation next week."

I found myself increasingly crazy with waiting for
Sunday. Would he even show up? Had I dreamed the
night before?

We met Tobe in a plaza where the bus stopped close
to the church. His eyes still looked puffy from sleep.
He smiled, sheepishly at first, then with a huge grin
that took in Nancy, Cathy, and me.

"I'm so glad to see you," was all I could muster.

"We were afraid you'd chicken out," Cathy filled in.

Tobe just laughed. In the courtyard of the church,
people stared at him as usual.

"The pastor speaks Spanish very clearly," I cued Tobe in. He was on my turf now, and I could show him around. After the service, a couple of old women made sure they shook Tobe's hand. The youth invited us to go on their usual walk with them.

"I've got to get back home for Sunday dinner," Tobe replied. "Momma made me promise to come home. Sunday *comida* is a really big deal," he explained.

"I know," I smiled. "I know. But why don't you come up to Tibidabo after siesta, and we can go to the amusement park?"

"Anything to be with you," Tobe whispered, out of the earshot of the others.

My face went hot; my heart raced like an engine idling too high. "Okay. See you."

"I'll come by the residencia as soon as I can get away."

It was a beautiful Sunday afternoon; I was so glad to have someone to go out with. We took the old New Orleans-style streetcar to the end of its line, then transferred to the cog car that climbed the rest of the mountain.

"This is gorgeous, isn't it?" Tobe pushed out his legs full length in the car that was practically empty except for a pregnant woman and her husband. "You've heard the story about how this is the mountain where Jesus was tempted, haven't you?" I asked.

"No."

"Our professor told us legend says that when Satan took Jesus up to a high point to look at all the kingdoms that could be his, this was where he stood."

Tobe's eyes crinkled in a smile. I nestled comfortably beside him, my shoulder just fitting under his arm. On Tibidabo we rode silly rides, ate deep-fried *churros,* and had the chicken that was a speciality on Tibidabo, almost like barbecued chicken.

Too soon the park closed, and we caught the last tram down from the mountain. The same couple was in our little compartment. The wife looked exhausted, but the husband was clearly celebrating, bringing out a *tirron* of wine in a leather pouch from their picnic bag now and then.

"So you're going to have a baby," Tobe motioned to the wife's tummy.

"Sí, sí," the husband replied proudly.

"When is you baby due?" I struggled to find the proper Spanish.

The wife brightened. "In two months, June."

Tobe seemed pleased that I'd entered the conversation. "I'm Tobe, and this is my girlfriend, Melodie."

"And I'm José, and this is my wife Angel."

Tobe was always finding someone to practice his Spanish on like that. Before I knew it, he and the husband were calling each other *paisano,* which means something like "brother" or "fellow countryman."

"Here, have a drink from my tirron," José offered. "I bet you can't even hit your mouth!"

A tirron has a long, narrow spout like on a watering can. You try to direct the liquid from the spout into your mouth. Tobe missed at first, then got it right. They took turns until they were both quite light-headed.

"Let's have a drink together before we say good-bye," Tobe suggested as we got off the streetcar near the Rotunda Hotel's coffee shop which I frequented.

141

"Sure." José was giddy. We women ordered coffee, but the men asked for cognacs, joking and slapping each other on the back like old army buddies. Angel and I tried to think of things to say. She was small and attractive, yet clearly from the working-class of Barcelona. She was quite different from the young women at the residencia who were pursuing careers in pharmacy or architecture.

"Will you two be godparents for our child?" Tobe asked José, then winked at me.

"What," I mouthed, "are you doing?"

Tobe motioned for me to play along.

"Godparents, sí sí," said José. "If you two will be godparents for our little one."

"Did you hear that, Melodie?" Tobe was triumphant. "We're going to be godparents!"

"Okay, sure," I agreed.

"This calls for a drink!" We all toasted each other.

"Would you like to come see where we live?" Angel invited.

Tobe looked at me. "Sure, why not?"

By this time it appeared that José would need help walking anyway, and he was in no condition to be leaning on a pregnant wife. We caught their bus which, after going miles toward nowhere, dumped us in a neighborhood far outside the city.

"Iss not far now." José's words were slurred. "But I want to take you to favorite bar. Wonderful place. You must see."

By this time I was growing impatient. It was already 11:00, and I was concerned about how we would get back to our section of Barcelona. Where were we, anyway?

142

The bar was a perfect specimen of authentic Spain, with hams and sausages hanging all over and a guitar player strumming near the back. I was sure that it had never been stepped into by a tourist before, it was that out of the way. People stared openly at Tobe and me.

"You'll have to spend the night with us," Angel invited cheerily as we left the bar.

"Oh, we couldn't trouble you with that," I said politely.

"We have an extra room and everything." She looked at me with a big smile. "It won't be any trouble."

"No, really, we can't stay," I said, looking at Tobe for help. He was grinning. Had he put them up to this? "Tobe's family and my roommates will wonder where we are."

If Tobe had let on to the husband that we were looking for a place to sleep, he was only supportive of my protests now.

"Yes, I must take Melodie home," he said. "But first let's just see their apartment."

In an aside to me, he whispered, "You're always saying you wish you could get into more Spanish homes."

The whole apartment was barely larger than one good-sized room. It consisted of a kitchen, living room, and two bedrooms so small you had to crawl over the bed to get in. The bathroom was out on the roof, shared, I suppose, with several other families.

But Angel was showing me around like it was a penthouse suite. They served us coffee and cookies in the living room. Finally I insisted again that we really had to go.

"But the buses aren't running any longer," José pointed out. "You'll have to walk."

"Well, how can we get to the Metro?" I asked, frustration rising.

"That's closed, too. You'll have to stay here."

I looked to Tobe for help. "We'll call a taxi," he offered.

The man just looked at him. "Out here, at this hour? It will cost a fortune."

My heart sank. Maybe the only wise thing to do was just stay here, then take the earliest Metro home so my roommates wouldn't know I'd stayed out all night. They'd never believe my story.

"Okay, we'll stay," I said finally, whispering to Tobe that one of us would have to sleep on the couch.

Angel was struggling in her pregnant state to make up the bed that you couldn't walk around. "The first night, you have to celebrate," she explained.

"Oh we're not going to sleep together."

I was embarrassed, but she acted like making a "first night" bed for us was a perfectly normal thing to do. Perhaps it was. There was an old tradition in Spain that directed young women to make the bed for a pair of newlyweds.

"It's one more symbol of the control and ever-present eye of the community," Professor Maria Angeles had told us as we shook our heads.

Now Angel looked at me like *I* was crazy. Tobe—so tall, so good-looking, so masculine. A free private bed.

"But why not?"

"I just don't believe in sex before marriage," I tried to explain.

She sat down on the bed. "Look," she said like an older sister. "It's not such a sin, really. We slept together before we were married, and sex is much better then. More spontaneous."

I looked at her stomach. Maybe sex was harder for her now, at seven months along. How sad, I thought, to really feel that the best sex could only happen before marriage.

I shook my head. "The first time I sleep with a man, I want it to be with the blessings and good wishes of all my friends and family after a wedding," I said.

My daydream of driving away on my honeymoon while friends peppered us with rice flitted through my mind. How *special* that would be, to come to one's first night of marriage with no regrets.

Angel looked at me a bit wistfully, then said, "If you don't want to sleep together, we obviously can't make you. I'll make up the sofa bed in the living room."

"You don't have to do that," I cried, sorry for all the work we were making her. She looked older than the 25 some years she probably was. "Tobe said he would sleep on the couch."

"No, no, he mustn't," Angel insisted. "It wouldn't be right not to give our guests the best we have."

I sighed, knowing it was a useless fight. Mother would never believe this. I felt like a hostage, held against my will.

Everyone was finally settled for the night. But sleep was far, far away after all the coffee, let alone this bizarre situation of hospitality carried too far. I started shivering, then trembled in huge, terrible quakes like you get with a high fever.

145

"Melodia," Tobe called softly at the door, using my Spanish name.

"Yes, come in," I whispered.

He wedged himself in the corner of the tiny room. I suddenly giggled at the idea of even thinking of sleeping with such a big guy in a bed less than twin size.

"Are you okay?" he asked gently.

"Yes, I'm f-f-fine," I stuttered.

"Then why are you shaking?"

"I don't know."

He shook his head. "I'm sorry I got you into this."

"Did you hint to José that you wanted to sleep with me or something?"

"No, no, honest. I don't know where they got that idea. Just a natural assumption, I guess. Of course it's true, but not unless you'd want to."

I wanted to, that wasn't the point. For a moment, I considered it. What a temptation! Who would know, besides this couple who had encouraged us? Complete privacy. No worry about parent. I knew part of the reason I was trembling was that I *did* want Tobe. Maybe if one clung to a value long enough, it *would* carry one through a vulnerable moment like this.

"No, let's not. I'm okay, really. I'll be fine."

He kissed me gently. Inside I felt a new surge of tenderness for a guy who didn't push his way with me.

"Good night, Melodie."

"Yeah, good night."

He closed the door, but I still couldn't sleep. Slowly I became aware that my bladder was terribly, horribly full after all the coffee, even though I had used the bathroom when Angel had showed it to me.

146

I tried the back door. It was locked, of course. I searched for a key. Should I wake the Fernandezes? It was now 2:00 a.m. After all the trouble we had caused them (or was it the trouble they had caused us), I simply couldn't wake Angel now. I would have to wait.

But I couldn't sleep. Three o'clock rolled around. I was bursting. If I had had my fun, now I was paying for it. I knew suddenly that if something terrible happened and I somehow wound up in hell, my punishment would be having an eternally full bladder and no place to relieve myself.

I heard the roosters start crowing about 4:30. We were close enough to the country that apparently some folks kept chickens. Morning wasn't far off. Mr. Fernandez had said he'd leave about 5:30 to walk to the Metro to get to his job by 6:30.

At last I heard stirrings. I went out and sheepishly asked if I could use the bathroom. A beautiful day was dawning, but I felt like I'd just crammed all night. I literally had not slept a wink.

We walked to the Metro in silence. José and Tobe exchanged phone numbers, and Tobe promised to visit after the baby was born. I wasn't sure I ever wanted to see them again.

About 6:30, I crawled in through the windows at the residencia where we'd heard the serenade. My bed never looked so good.

What was I going to do about Tobe? What would Mom and Dad say when I told them I thought I was falling in love with a black guy? Why should I even tell them his color? I wouldn't if he were white.

Even with the tumble of these thoughts on my mind, I was soon asleep.

147

15

Spring Break

It never occurred to me that, while I was worrying about what to tell Mom and Dad, Tobe was worrying about what his mom and dad would think of me.

"I don't know exactly what or how much to say," I said in my letter home, "or how soon my mind will change completely. But I really want to tell you about a nice guy I've been seeing . . ."

I finished with: "You'd like him, Mom. Reminds me of Sidney Poitier with his old-fashioned charm and gentlemanliness."

This was all their fault, I told myself with a chuckle. They brought me up with all colors of people in our home. They told me, "We don't care what color man you marry as long as he's Christian."

In some ways I was glad I had planned to leave the country for spring break, with airline tickets to London already in hand. The days since I had met Tobe had become intense, mind-bending. I knew that, even though I'd miss him, it would be good to take a breather from our relationship and get some perspective.

We spent all the evenings together before my departure. One night we went out for sandwiches and talked for hours. I learned that his father drove taxi in St. Louis, Missouri. Tobe lived there (instead of New York as he had first told me) in a middle-class house.

After two years of high school in St. Louis, he dropped out. Then, because of his athletic skills, he was accepted at an exclusive Andover, Massachusetts, prep school. He had only spent the past summer in New York City, working as a swimming and basketball coach at a community center. There he had come into contact with drug addicts and street people.

His senior year he was spending in Barcelona, but he would graduate back in the States in June. This meant he was only 19 rather than 20, another fact he had to correct now. He was hoping to study history and political science in college and had always dreamed of being a lawyer. But he was less sure now after his New York experience. Maybe he would be a counselor of some kind.

"I'm sure you'll end up somehow working with people," I told him. "You're a natural."

"Yeah?"

"Everyone likes you—you just know how to make people feel at home."

He grinned again, then got very serious and took my hand.

"Melodie, I've been doing a lot of thinking. I want you to marry me."

My heart stopped, then raced ahead double time. His face told me he wasn't joking. The question was obviously premature, at least to my mind, yet I didn't want to hurt him or rule out the future.

"Oh, Tobe," I said, "We've only known each other a little more than a week. I learned more about you tonight than I did in all our other times together. I just don't know yet."

"Can't you just see the little girl we'd have?"

"Wa-wa-wa-wait a minute," I stammered. "I haven't even said I'd marry you. Now you're talking babies?"

He laughed.

"Okay, so maybe I'm getting ahead of myself." Tobe shook his head. "I just don't want to lose you."

"Nobody's losing anyone. Just give it time," I felt like a mother.

"You're going to be gone so long."

"Well, just twelve days, and then *you'll* be gone." Tobe's study group was spending spring break traveling to Galacia and Basque country.

"I know; that's what makes it really long."

"It might be good for us."

From a street vendor, Tobe bought me a single red rose. There was more than just this good-bye hanging between us. We were also thinking ahead to our good-bye in June.

"Have you thought any more about my question?" Tobe asked as we rode the Metro north to my residencia.

"Your question," I stalled. He looked hurt. "Oh, yes, your *question*."

I turned to face him. "I haven't thought of anything else," I said huskily. "It blows my mind—not just that you want to marry me, but that you're ready to ask so soon."

"So that means no."

"No, just 'wait.' Be patient. Maybe I can tell you something when I come back from London."

He sighed. We climbed up the steps of the Metro and walked silently to his bus stop. It was only two blocks to my residencia.

"Well, make sure you do think about it," Tobe reminded, as he finally tore himself away to board his bus. He looked at me till the bus turned out of sight, like a little boy going off for his first day of school.

Anita and I met early the next day to depart for London from the Barcelona airport. It was like reverse culture shock to land in London's busy Heathrow airport and see signs in English, hear English, and best of all, communicate without a second thought.

We found a cheap, student dorm-type place, and got oriented by taking a tourist's typical tour of London. "Notice that all the flags on top of the buildings are at half-mast," said the tour guide, "because of the death of Pompidou."

One woman, who had been very talkative, blurted out, "Who is Pompidou?"

When all of us turned around to see who had been hibernating the last several days since the death of France's president, she shrugged her shoulders. "Hey, I have to work all day long," she said. "I don't have time to read, you know."

I was glad to note from her accent, with a bit of surprise, that she was English. So not only people from my country, myself included, could be woefully uninformed.

I felt so out of touch with all that was happening with the Watergate crisis. There had been something in the Spanish papers about 1,200 pages of tape transcripts being subpoenaed. Was it true? We eagerly gobbled up the London papers. They seemed somehow more believable, if only because they were in English.

We met the students from my college whom we had arranged to meet in London. (They were in Europe on a 14-week term.) They assured us it was all true and worse. Nixon would surely resign even if he wasn't impeached. Impeach? Resign? What was happening to the integrity of that office? To my country?

By day we hit most of London's tourist spots. Evenings we went to the theaters, just so we'd have a chance to sit down. It was a veritable, mind-boggling feast: *Godspell, Streetcar Named Desire, Jesus Christ Superstar.*

We saw Stravinsky's *Rite of Spring* ballet in the Royal Opera House, feeling rather dingy in jeans and not having had time to wash. Everyone else seemed to be arriving in limos and tuxedos. All of this almost made me forget it was also Easter weekend, but I was thrilled to end up at St. Paul's Cathedral on Easter Sunday morning. High church on Christianity's most holy day!

But it was in walking the streets that I grasped the real world Christ died for. It seemed like literally every country of the world was represented on London's streets. There were restaurants to match, especially from Asia, India, and the Middle East.

It was impossible to decipher all the languages. The atmosphere was utterly cosmopolitan, and I reveled in it. Here was a place Tobe and I would not be stared at, just as we would not be stared at in many large cities in

152

North America. Maybe I could think about saying yes to his question after all.

Our last evening we were so exhausted we returned to our dismal quarters early to take care of essentials like washing our hair and packing. I tried not to stare at Anita's pelvic bones protruding from her sides. She had begun the year weighing about the same as me. Now she was an almost anorexic 105 pounds.

"How did you manage to lose so much weight this year?"

"I couldn't stand all the oil our señora used in her cooking. It made my stomach upset. When you can't eat the cooking, you lose weight." Anita shrugged.

"Didn't she get offended?" I asked. "I've heard others say that it's so hard to turn down the food their 'mothers' cook."

"Yes, she's terribly hurt. That's why she doesn't like me much. You were lucky to get in the residencia."

"I guess so. Funny how things work out."

"I mean I was so *glad* when you all volunteered. Especially when I found out what some of the other girls were like."

I guessed she was referring to Nancy's charismatic enthusiasm.

"You know, Anita," I began, trusting her enough now to bare this part of my self. "I guess you could tell that my friends from EMC were a lot more like you and Nonda [Anita's best friend] than Nancy and the others. Last year I lived in a house with a bunch of guys and girls who were—you know, really into living in community, and a just society, and all the things you're majoring in. I really liked them and got interested in the issues that fascinated them."

153

Anita listened thoughtfully. "I don't always agree with where Nancy and Bonnie come out," I went on, "but I've really learned to love them, too. Somehow my whole understanding of what it means to be a Christian has widened. I've even gotten to the place where I now believe there are Christians in the military."

"How can you stand those Navy guys who come into Barcelona? Some of them were trying to hit on me and Nonda the other night. We told them to get lost."

I couldn't explain myself, partly because some of my feelings were so new to me, partly because I was just too tired. Perhaps I was beginning to see that in my confusion over my upbringing and some of my new learnings, there was a middle ground. Perhaps what I needed was not to lean too far either left *or* right. Instead, I needed to find some undefined, difficult *third* way. It did feel good to count Anita as a new friend.

At Heathrow Airport we joined other people from Spain waiting for the flight back to Barcelona. It was a barnyard. The line to check our baggage moved terribly slowly. The Spanish travelers pushed and squeezed up against me like ornery sows in Dad's pig pen.

We had gotten so used to being shoved and pushing others ourselves in Barcelona. But after spending twelve days in the land of the proper British, this inclination to pack like pigs infuriated me. It was really only the cultural difference of Spaniards feeling comfortable with less distance between people than I was used to, but it still angered me.

Perhaps it was this rude reawakening that made me

depressed on the trip back to Barcelona. After such a feast of culture, was I a better person? Maybe having seen all the "in" plays and knowing how to talk about impressionist paintings or famous composers weren't the most important things in life. Was it possible to soak up too much culture, so that one became "cultured" like buttermilk—and smelly? I've observed that cultured people sometimes held up their noses as if they were smelling something bad.

Perhaps it was all the work awaiting me back in Barcelona, the end-of-the-school year run for the goal line. Perhaps it was Tobe's question hanging over me. What would I tell him? Maybe it was knowing that I wouldn't see him for another week and that with his charm he probably wasn't without female companionship.

It *was* unexpectedly good to hear Spanish again, almost as good as hearing English on arriving in London. Here were Anita and I—the girls at the very bottom of the class (in language) at the beginning of the year. Now we understood practically every word. We smiled like conspirators, overhearing some Spanish guys discussing us: "Americans—or are they English?" They were assuming we couldn't understand a word.

As the plane landed, I felt like I was really home. But I also faced the terrible knowledge that the end of my time in Spain was pushing on me as forcefully as a plane screaming to a stop.

16

Homestretch

Why did the fun always seem to start just when it was time to go home? I raced to pack into my remaining months as much Spanish life as possible.

Over spring break, Nancy had decided to finish up her classes early and leave for home by May 3. I dug into my papers immediately; after Tobe got back from his break, I'd have less time for studying.

Tara told us the American Institute where she tutored was looking for more tutors for Spanish students at about $2.60 an hour. It hardly seemed worthwhile to get started now. But if someone could use a tutor for six weeks, I could use the extra money. I started to feel overwhelmed. But then, the ends of all school years are like that—mad.

I still hadn't heard what my parents thought of my relationship with Tobe, even though I had written several letters and told them of his proposal.

Finally the hoped-for, yet dreaded, letter came. Mother went on and on about my application for financial aid for the coming college year, summer job possibilities, and local gossip.

Finally she got to the point. "It feels different when 'guess who's coming to dinner' happens at your own house," she began with faint humor. She then launched into the toughest letter I had ever received from her.

"You may want to chop my neck off because I'm sticking it out. You said you wanted an honest reaction. Why can't you find a nice Mennonite guy to settle down with? What kind of Christian is one who says he's a Christian in his 'own way'? What *is* he like, anyway? You seem to gloss over any real information about him."

Mom went on to ask if we had thought about where we would live; she said that we would surely have more problems than other couples and would always feel out of place with each others' relatives.

"Just be sure you count the cost of marrying someone like Tobe," she said in closing. "You've been hurt in love so often—I don't want you hurt again. You asked me to be honest so I'm laying my cards on the table."

I was devastated. Never before had I, a "good" daughter, done anything to disappoint my parents in a major way. How dare they put up so many red flags when they had always claimed to be so open? But I knew not only the hard questions had angered me. I was also mad because she had put her finger on issues I was trying to avoid—especially Tobe's relationship to Christ.

Deb knew I was upset. "Bad letter?" she asked.

"Now I know a little of . . . what it feels like to have your parents really upset with you, like you were saying about your parents."

"Tobe?"

"Yeah, Tobe."

Concha came in the room from her classes and sat down. She pulled out a cigarette, then offered me one out of habit, though I always turned her down. If the Spanish were not shy about borrowing things, neither were they stingy.

"Thanks" I said, pulling a cigarette from her pack. If my parents were disappointed in me, I might as well be really "bad." I lit it feeling self-conscious and wicked. I had watched so many friends light up that it seemed almost natural.

"I was just telling Deb that Mom had finally written about Tobe," I explained. Concha lifted an eyebrow, then looked at Deb.

"When am I going to get to meet Tobe, anyway?"

"Yeah," Deb chimed in. "I've never seen him up close either."

"Okay, okay, when he comes tomorrow night, I'll think up a way you all can see him better."

Tobe wore a shy grin when we finally got to see each other. He was tall enough that I fit smoothly under his arms, like the right piece in a puzzle. How good it was to be hugged again.

"Some girls are dying to see you up closer," I whispered, motioning to the residencia. "Why don't we go get some pastries from the bakery and take them to Concha and Deb?"

"Sure," he said, "then I've got some people who are dying to meet you. I thought I could take you to see my family tonight. The little girl and boy were unhappy when I left after just getting back."

158

Deb mouthed, "He passes," after we'd delivered the pastries. Concha just smiled and said, as if in an English class, "I'm pleased to meet you."

My welcome at Tobe's "home" was less certain, at least from the little girl. The mother was more than gracious, but the four-year-old kept whispering, "When is *she* (me) going to leave?"

We tried to be alone in the apartment's small living room, but little sister and brother kept peeking in. Finally Tobe said, "I think I'd better take you home, then come back and pay some attention to the children."

"You passed one test." Tobe smiled merrily after we'd left. "I asked 'Mom' what she thought of you. She thought you were very nice."

"I'll bet. Coming in there and making her little girl all jealous!"

"Well, she wants you to come back for dinner sometime. I've told her I've asked you to marry me, you know."

"You didn't!"

"Well, you know she's just like a real mom to me. So have you decided yet?"

"I was afraid you were going to ask that."

"And I was afraid you were going to say that."

"So why'd you ask?"

"I just want to know where I stand."

"Have you thought about where we'd live? Obviously not any of the small towns I come from."

"I don't know. Maybe South America, where we could teach our little girls Spanish!"

"Really? For a long time I've dreamed of maybe living in South America too."

He looked at me incredulously. "You're not just saying that? Maybe we were meant to be together," Tobe said softly.

"There's something I've gotta know before I can ever begin to answer your question," I said finally. "I've gotta know if you really and truly—for yourself, are a Christian. Not just saying it to please me."

He was quiet a long time. "Yes, Melodie, I believe in Jesus," he said tiredly, like a father telling a child something for the tenth time.

"I'm far from perfect, you know that. And I have a lot of questions. Like when I was growing up, Jesus was always shown to us as a white man, you know. I have trouble seeing Jesus as white."

"Well he wasn't white or black, of course, kinda brown."

"Yeah, I know. But I identify with him more if I think of him as my color."

"Which *is* kind of brown."

Tobe ignored that. "I mean, if Jesus was perfect, and they showed me a white Jesus, that means white is somehow better than black because the only perfect man who ever lived was supposedly white."

For the first time I realized Tobe really had thought a lot about how he viewed Christ. He was trying to cope with his questions, like all young adults.

"Well, back to your proposal," I said, so he wouldn't have to bring it up again. "What I'd really like is for you to stop asking me to marry you."

Tobe looked confused.

"See, I just don't know yet, but I still want to go on being friends with you, going out with you. You're so good for me."

"What do you mean?"

"Well, you keep me from holing up in my room. I talk more Spanish when I'm out with you, because you're always getting me into situations where I have to talk Spanish. And you're teaching me so much about . . . about. . . ."

"About what it's like in the real world?" he laughed. "You're not going to be Mom and Dad's same little girl when you go back home, are you?"

It was true. I would never be the same. I had departed from so many of the absolutes I had been brought up on. Yet not all—and something in me kept asking troubling questions about the drinks that had increased in my social life with Tobe. And now smoking. But wasn't it a sign of friendship to accept a cigarette offered by someone else in this culture? Wasn't it one way to show I didn't consider myself somehow better than they?

I thought back to the night we had been invited to the sad, one-room apartment of a friend of one of Tobe's friends. He was an exiled El Salvadoran, a political refugee, I suppose, who was drowning his troubles that night in booze. The more he drank, the more disgusted I got, to the point of insisting to Tobe that we leave. This guy had fallen on the floor, passed out from drink. Tobe's other friend, a well-to-do ambassador's kid, left without even attempting to thank our host.

Tobe carefully turned off the stereo, cleared clutter off the bed, gathered up the young man and tucked him into bed, then turned off the light.

"I'll see you tomorrow, my friend," Tobe called into the darkness.

I was touched. If Tobe's one friend was the Levite, then I was the priest, and both of us were too good to dirty ourselves to help someone who was drunk. Tobe, in this case, was literally the good Samaritan—and of a "hated" race. I, who knew the parables so well I could immediately see modern-day parallels, had forgotten how to apply them.

Still, there had to be a line, didn't there, between really being involved with people and knowing when to say no? "Does someone have to sleep with a prostitute to show he cares for her?" I rhetorically asked my journal.

Nancy's goodbye party was a celebration of friendship. I hated to see her go but knew she would be happier once she could be with Mickey. She had often admitted her need to be "taken care of." She had held out until *almost* the end of the year—one could hardly call her a quitter now.

We brought in pizzas and toasted Nancy, each other, and everyone's boyfriend. Then someone had the idea of doing practical jokes—like the one where you smoke the bottom side of a lid or mirror with a candle, then have another person copy your moves as you rub your hand on the underside of a clean lid. Your unsuspecting partner rubs her hand in soot and slowly applies it, like makeup, to her face.

It was fun to see how many jokes were the same from culture to culture. What fine friends we had become!

We saw Nancy off at the bus station. "Good-bye, good-bye," I said, giving Nancy a Spanish-style kiss on both cheeks. "Say 'hi' to Mickey for us. Write."

Tears streamed down her bright, pink cheeks. They always got that way when she was excited. "Oh I will, I will." I knew that, with Nancy, it was not just an empty promise. She had faithfully written to friends in the States all year.

"Invite us to your wedding," Cathy joked. Nancy's blue eyes glistened. Then she was gone.

So the process of leaving had already been set in motion. No, it had begun long before that—even on the very day we left the States. We knew the day to go back would eventually come, even as the process of dying is set in motion at the very moment life begins.

"How are your papers coming?" Cathy asked, switching us back to the present.

"Not so good. I just discovered I was going completely in the wrong direction. I didn't have enough material to make a paper. Now I have to start over."

"That's a bummer."

"But at least I discovered it earlier than the night before it was due or something."

"How do you like tutoring by now?" Cathy had been tutoring ever since Christmas break.

I laughed. "At first I didn't have a clue what I was doing. But then I discovered what he needed most was just to practice talking with someone in English. And he's helped me so much with my Spanish!"

"What do you mean?"

"Like he helped me understand why my Spanish pronunciation has always been so poor. That to talk Spanish properly you have to say the words up here in the front of your mouth, while we have the tendency to pronounce words down in our throats. And that's

163

also why Spanish people talking English sound so funny."

Cathy smiled, like it was a trick I should have learned long ago. And it was. But how long would it have escaped me if I hadn't had the tables reversed by trying to teach a Spanish man English!

Back at the residencia, I knew I had to tackle the paper that was headed in the wrong direction. I needed to prepare for the next tutoring session. I paced the floor of the study room like a cat, unable to concentrate. I wanted food but didn't want to eat.

Maybe I'd go and buy a pack of cigarettes so I wouldn't eat. I hurried to the corner tobacco store, where I'd only bought postage stamps before, and asked for a pack of cheap Spanish cigarettes.

Back in the room, I had smoked three before I knew it. My heart was racing like I'd just had five cups of coffee. I caught a whiff of my breath, and it reminded me of an old man who used to try to kiss me and my sisters when we were kids.

Suddenly I ground out the spark on the weed I was smoking. What was I doing? I didn't want to come home from Spain with a habit I couldn't break, and it was easy to see now how rapidly this could become a habit.

I settled on a different stimulant, coffee, and tried to concentrate. I found my mind wandering back to the previous night, when Tobe had found a wallet on the street. There was no money, but it held what looked like lots of important identification papers and cards. We tried to give it to a nearby police officer, but since we were near police headquarters, he directed us to go there.

The person on duty thanked us cordially and asked Tobe to leave his name and address in case the person wanted to give a reward. I had to think what might have happened in my home town if a black man and white woman had brought in a wallet stripped of its cash at 11:30 p.m.

At times, I had to admit, I was prejudiced too. Not about the lovely color of his skin, his fuzzy hair, or the snapping, black eyes. What annoyed me was his tendency to borrow money and "forget" to pay it back. There was the time he spent $10 treating all his friends to drinks, then later realized he could have bought the shoes he needed with that money.

There were jokes—even words, English words—I heard him use I didn't begin to understand. Like *nappy*. Or *jive*. And there were the lies he'd told me in the beginning. How did I know when he was telling me the truth?

"Why did you lie to me about your age when you first met me?" I asked one night.

"I was afraid you'd think I was too young."

"But now I don't know how I can be sure you're telling the truth instead of jiving me."

"Can't ever trust a nigger, can you?" Tobe had drunk more than he should have that night.

"I didn't say that."

"But it's there."

"Oh, sometimes I just don't know how we'd ever make it; it might be too hard." I choked, sobs overtaking my body at the thought of the difficulties inherent in our relationship.

"I know, baby." He hugged me. "I know."

"But we can keep trying to make it work. I love how you're making me face things in myself that I would never have admitted before."

In Tobe's arms I felt so beautiful. Somehow through him I again delighted in seeing tiny children. Somehow I wanted to love this man who cared so deeply about so many, who gave of himself without thinking of the consequences.

"I *want* to marry you," I went on, "but sometimes I just don't understand you. I wonder if I ever could. Like *how* can you go through money so fast?"

I had already seen him give his last peseta to a beggar on the street. He was the kind of person who lived so intensely he would probably die young for some useless reason. I shuddered at the thought.

"Listen to a drunk man, Melodie. A drunk man tells no lies," Tobe rambled. "Sometimes I think I'm just the biggest sucker there ever was."

Now he was really sounding drunk, the confessional kind of drunk when a man goes on and on about his troubles.

"Spell it with a capital 'S' if you like. But listen to me, Melodie. I'm such a sucker I'm gonna die young. You know it; in some strange way, we both know it. I can't explain it."

I practically gagged. It wasn't the first time the thought had occurred to me, but what kind of mental telepathy did we have, anyway? Like the feeling I'd had the day I met him that something special was about to happen.

My Christian background wanted to ask, "Well, are you ready to die?"

But I knew him well enough to know he would probably say, "All I know is what I feel in my heart. Yes, I'm ready, whatever that means."

Was he indeed a "sucker" or a beautiful human being? Could I really give up my upbringing and culture to join Tobe in his; could he join in mine? Was there a middle ground someplace where we could enjoy the best of each others' worlds?

My head felt like it would burst from thinking about it all. I felt like an octopus with eight legs pulling me in different directions. One of them was saying, like an observer: Enjoy this experience, Melodie. This is life! Enjoy these wonderful days of living so fully, in love with a guy and this new country.

There was no way I ever wanted to leave Spain or Tobe. Things would never be the same.

17

Going Home

My last weeks in Spain flew by. My presentation on the dehumanization of art (modern art movement) sounded intellectual even to me. My tutoring sessions with the English student were fun, and my papers got finished, one by one.

Letters from home came further and further apart. One day I was shocked to find one penned by Dad. He almost never writes letters. But he wrote that he still loved me, was praying for me, and was sure I'd make the right decision.

Time had worked its grace. Somehow they had cooled down about Tobe, just like I had. Mom shared how she had gone to visit Dad at his Civilian Public Service camp during the war even though her mom had forbid it. *WOW*, I thought. My mom a rebel? Why don't parents ever tell their kids how they disappointed their parents until the kids have somehow upset them?

One day there was a surprise sitting in the foyer of the residencia when I got back from classes. Marlin, a friend from my college in the States, was finishing up his term in Europe by traveling through Barcelona. He had decided to look me up.

I gave him a big bear hug and dispensed with studies for the rest of the night. Cathy and I took him for a quick tour of our favorite spots. We went to one of architect Antonio Gaudí's more famous works, the Sagrada Familia cathedral with its weird spires, as unfinished as the day Gaudí had died.

"No one knows how to complete it," I explained, "because he supposedly had the plans in his head and changed them each day as he went."

We also took Marlin to Park Guell—Gaudí's fantastically creative playground in northern Barcelona.

I was pleased to learn that two girls from the EMC group had sent word with Marlin that they would like me to rent an apartment with them back at school next year.

Without even wanting to, I was acknowledging with these plans that there would be life beyond Spain. Tobe had sent word to Brown University that he definitely would be enrolling there. How far was Rhode Island from Virginia?

Our departure date, June 7, was coming before the official end of the university school year. I needed to make arrangements to take exams in some of my classes or do alternate work. I wrote out a careful speech for Professor Marcos, explaining that I was a foreigner needing to leave before the scheduled exam. Could I write an extra paper? It was the first time all semester that I had talked with him, so I rehearsed every word. I didn't want to make a dumb mistake.

He smiled faintly, as if to say I needn't have informed him I was a foreigner. But he quickly agreed on an assigned topic for a paper. I was relieved to have one more going-home chore completed.

I packed all my winter clothes and the books I didn't need any more in a box and shipped them by freight, as advised by the Camans. While I was getting rid of things on one hand, I was also spending every spare moment shopping for souvenirs for family and friends.

I counted the days until my departure even as I relished each remaining moment. I savored the leisurely suppers in the room with Concha, Cynta, or whoever happened to be around; doing exercises; "taking coffee" together. These times no longer seemed wasted. They were precious, priceless, golden moments.

Tobe and I had unfinished business as well. "I thought we'd try to pay a visit to the Fernandezes," said Tobe one Saturday when we got together.

"Oh, I really don't want to," I protested. "What if they make us stay overnight again?"

"Come on," Tobe said laughing. "We promised we'd come see them again. Maybe they've had their baby."

We finally rode the bus out to the area where the Fernandezes lived and tried to find their apartment.

"All the streets look alike out here," I complained. But Tobe had their street address. Soon we were knocking on their door.

No answer. Knock, knock, knock. No answer. Tobe was genuinely disappointed. I was relieved. I just didn't want to see them again. Tobe left a note saying we had tried to visit.

"Let's get something to eat." Tobe took my hand.

"I'm hungry for calamares," I said. "Let's go to that little place close to the cathedral that sells them cheap."

We rode the buses back to where we could get a Metro for downtown and found the bar.

"Did I ever tell you how Paco first got me to eat these things?" I asked. "He kind of shamed me into it. He sure doesn't mind embarrassing someone," I said, holding up one of the fried squid for Tobe to look at. Tobe fed me one too, like a groom feeding his bride wedding cake.

Nearing the front of the cathedral, we heard the familiar strains of sardana music. We gathered around one of the circles to watch. The dancers solemnly linked arms with each other in a beautiful solidarity. They were proud Catalans who danced here every Saturday night and Sunday noon as if to keep the spirit of Catalonia alive despite Franco's demand that they speak a language not native to them.

Yet the circles were not closed to outsiders. When the song ended, the dancers dropped arms to rest for the next song. Before I knew it, an old man had asked Tobe and me if we wanted to learn the steps. He practiced with us to the side of the dancers, and in half an hour we had joined one of the circles.

I wasn't as smooth as Tobe. But bobbing together, arm in arm with these wonderful people, it was easy to forget a world where we wouldn't be welcomed as easily. Why couldn't folks all over the world join arms in one big circle regardless of language, color, beliefs?

171

Why couldn't we go on dancing forever, and not have to think of mundane things like what on earth would I do this summer for a job?

Tobe had been doing a little souvenir buying of his own. Rather simple—a little wooden heart necklace on which he had carved "Te quiero" (I love you) in Spanish, like a kid carving on a tree. We took last pictures of each other and got a passerby to photograph us together in Plaza Cataluña.

"I'll go crazy if I can't see you again," I pleaded. "You'll have to come down to Florida this summer and meet my parents and get that over with. I know they'll like you."

"It's not them I'm worried about. What would the people in town do to me seeing me with their 'homecoming attendant'?" he teased.

"I don't know. I don't care. All I know is I've got to see you again after Spain, on my home turf."

But at least he had stopped asking me to marry him. I liked the confidence this evidenced; having a guy falling all over himself for me had always been a big turnoff.

"I have real peace about us," I told Tobe. "I know there'd be problems, but I'm not worried about them. I've asked God for guidance, and whatever will happen, will happen." But already I wondered if I'd ever hear anything from Tobe, once he got back with *his* old friends, after the many hearts he'd surely broken earlier. And he was going off to an ivy league school as an impressionable freshman.

There were so many things I wanted to do one last time—have the thick chocolate drink *suizo* with churros, feed the pigeons in Plaza Cataluña, plus just saying good-bye to various friends.

The sending-off party for our group was planned for the same night as Tobe's. Although he invited me to theirs, I felt I should be with my own study group.

We went to a restaurant and had pizzas and round upon round of drinks, toasts. Finally Paco got up to make his speech.

"You've been a good group," he began. I marveled that he had either slowed his speech tremendously in the course of the year, or I had really gotten better at understanding it. "But you haven't been as close as last year's," he went on. Spanish candor, or was that a stereotype?

"I'm not saying that's bad," Paco continued. "The group last year stuck together so much I'm afraid they didn't do as good a job as you as making Spanish friends."

We all relaxed. I thought of Tara and her friends. Deb and Concha. Bonnie and her friends at church. Lydia from Calle Verdi who had helped me with my language problems whenever I asked. Conchita and Cynta, Vicki, Tonia—lots of girls I had gotten to know at least a little. Several of the guys had developed good Spanish friends. It was true. We *had* gotten to know more than just the kids in the group.

Back at the residencia, I stepped out onto the balcony upstairs as I prepared for bed. I took a deep breath. It smelled, of all things, like the summer camp I went to as a girl. Woodsy and verdant, with a full moon making it perfect. A moon as full as my heart.

How could I hold onto this year, this flight toward

173

independence, this fairy-tale life? Soon the magic would end. I would be just Cinderella again, working in who knows what kind of a job for the summer. Maybe I'd end up being a maid again, like I had been one summer, instead of having my own maid.

Tobe was to leave Barcelona three days before Deb, Cathy, and I would catch a bus to Paris. Cathy and I went to see Tobe's bus off, as she had remained casual friends with one of his friends. Soon all there was time for was one last kiss, one last embrace, then one last look. Tobe was gone.

Cathy knew not to say much, not to look me square in the eyes for a good long time after we left the bus station. Yet I was glad for her companionship, glad I hadn't had to face this alone. He was gone.

"I'm so happy your Mom and Dad agreed to come get us in New York," I said finally. "Isn't that a long drive?"

"Sure, but how often does your only daughter come back from living abroad?" Cathy joked.

"Really. And then to offer to take me to the Baltimore airport yet so I can fly on home. You have *some* parents."

"I know. I'm just glad you're going to get to stay with me a day so I can introduce you to all my friends and take you out for some good Pennsylvania cooking."

"I just want a hamburger. Good old made-in-the-USA hamburger."

"Cokes that don't cost an arm and a leg."

"French fries not cooked with olive oil."

We laughed, preparing ourselves for reverse cultural shock. Nancy was gone, now Tobe was too. Cathy and I were left, just like at the beginning of the year when had hit it off together.

The next two days were anti-climactic, with time suspended. I felt like I'd already left for home, with Tobe gone. We said final good-byes to Conchita, the señora of the residencia. We bid fond farewells to the folks at church, this sweetened by the fact that Christians never really have to say good-bye.

I walked alone through the Gothic quarters one last time, feeling like Emily in *Our Town*. I desperately wanted to tell the people on the streets, "Do you know that in three days I'll be in the United States? Can't you see? Don't you know how lucky you are to live here in this lovely city of artists and poets and flower vendors on every corner? Do you enjoy the splendor that is yours here, today?"

For my last night at the residencia what should appear in the stained glass window on the stairway but a lizard—right there with the representation of St. George. I smiled at the homely lizard. Maybe St. George *had* helped me slay my giants this year—language, homesickness, procrastination, struggles with loneliness and with wanting a relationship with a guy. Even the lizard had come to say good-bye.

Our trip home began on June 7 on the overnight bus to Paris. We arrived at midday, and I wanted to get a hotel. But Cathy and Deb thought it would be easier just to take our stuff to the airport and sleep there.

We were a picture, especially when we got stranded in traffic in the middle of the Champs Elysees. There were crazy Paris drivers streaming everywhere, while

175

we ferried our luggage from one side of the wide boulevard to the other in shifts.

We felt like bag ladies as we tried to sleep on the floor of the restroom because it was warmest there. We were chased out by the cleaning woman. The airport chairs were so uncomfortable!

After several delays, at long last we were on the flight home. Before I knew it, a flight attendant touched my arm.

"We'll be landing soon. Please fasten your seatbelt."

"Will your family be meeting you in New York?" my seatmate was asking. Deb, Cathy, and I had been separated on the nearly full plane.

"The parents of one of the girls I'm traveling with will," I said politely to the woman in her double-knit, "traveling to Europe" suit.

"That's good," she said, motherlike, but I didn't mind.

"Look, look, there's the Statue of Liberty," the woman said. So it was, standing so proudly in the harbor, welcoming me home. I couldn't believe it. Tears edged my eyes. I wasn't supposed to feel patriotic about seeing the Statue of Liberty. I had been raised to feel *uncomfortable* if I slid my hand over my heart to be like everyone else when the "Star Spangled Banner" was sung; now I was feeling (to echo columnist Meg Greenfield) something red, white, and blue about coming home.

But where was home? Part of me was still on the other side of the Atlantic, part of me was in the Midwest somewhere with Tobe. Maybe it was okay to love my country after all, just as I knew Cynta and Concha

176

and all the others loved theirs, in spite of its flaws. Maybe it was really true that the Christian is never truly at home on this earth, a sojourner here from the heavenly land.

New York's skyscrapers jabbed me back to the here and now, like the electric prod Dad used to use on the pigs. The plane dropped and began its final descent to the airport.

"I'm really home," I said to myself, tears damming, then spilling from my eyes. Then—whether due to the sudden change in altitude, the fact that I'd been traveling almost three days without decent sleep, or the weight of all the ways I'd let myself and God down in this year abroad—a dam burst inside my nose and soul. Blood, blood, and more blood came flowing till I'd used up all my tissues and the stewardess brought me more.

"I don't know what's the matter with me," I apologized to my seatmate, sniffing and wiping both my eyes and my nose. "But isn't it great to be back home?"

"I know, dearie, I know," the double-knit suit said, patting my hand. But I didn't care anymore what either of us was wearing.

In customs, a huge man mechanically processed my passport. But before I could even think the words "humph—friendly government bureaucracy," he met my eyes and boomed out a hearty, "Welcome home!" I felt like hugging him. It *was* great to be home, but now I wanted some sleep.

18

Aftershock

"Just look at all the tall guys!" Cathy squealed. We linked arms out of Spanish habit as we walked through JFK Airport.

"Yeah, and did you notice their pants are loose enough they can actually move!"

Cathy laughed, then suddenly realized we were no longer in Spain and sheepishly dropped my arm from hers.

In the baggage claim area I exclaimed, "Look, how orderly everyone is—no one pushing and shoving!"

Cathy's mother had prepared a tailgate supper for us to eat in the parking lot before heading for Lancaster County. So my first meal back in the States was not the long-fantasized hamburger but egg salad sandwiches, veggies, and chips—and for dessert, whoopie pies!

"Just like *my* mom makes!" I told Mrs. Bewley approvingly. It wasn't quite McDonald's. But, in its homemade way, it was all the more tasty and welcoming.

"Can you believe how big the cars look?" Cathy asked. The skyrocketing oil prices of 1973-74 had not yet hit the average car owner. Most people were still driving big old boats—especially compared to the compacts which were *all* you saw in Spain. A big Buick on the streets of Barcelona attracted as much attention as a limousine on the streets of Blountstown.

Mr. Bewley stopped for gas, and Cathy and I did another double take. We had heard the price of gas had risen astronomically, but it was something else to actually see the prices for ourselves. "How can people afford such high-priced gas?" I asked Mr. Bewley.

He laughed and said, "Oh, people cut back in their driving for awhile, but we soon get used to anything in this country."

"Do you think Nixon will really be impeached?" I went on, eager to be updated on the scandal that had seemed so distant across the sea.

"I don't know. Maybe he'll resign first. Were people talking about it in Spain?"

"Some," I said. "Mostly we never knew what to believe in the papers. If the paper said Nixon would resign I thought, that's just the Spanish press."

The need for sleep soon overtook my desire to get caught up. When we arrived at Cathy's home, she took me for a quick tour and checked out the family-owned greenhouse and floral shop. Then she showed me the shower and a twin bed. When I crawled into bed after three days of not seeing one, it felt so good I didn't wake up for twelve hours.

When I was finally on the plane for Tallahassee, it hit me that in saying good-bye to Cathy, my last link to

Spain was severed. Cathy had first befriended me, had seen me through my worst times in Spain and some of my best, had been with me when I met as well as said good-bye to Tobe. Now she was one more memory. But we had already made tentative plans to visit each other at our schools in the coming year.

From the plane I peered down at the slim road shooting west out of Tallahassee, through the miles of pine trees that would take me on the final leg of my long journey home. Were Mom and Dad already at the airport? I hoped my only brother, Terry, had come along too. It would be so good to see him. And I wouldn't cry again. I had cried enough over New York's harbor.

But waiting to get off the plane, walking down the ramp behind the too-slow crowds, my throat grew thick. Only five months had elapsed since I had put Mom and Dad on a plane in Barcelona. Yet those months had put our relationship through the greatest strain we had experienced. I knew they still loved me—but would Dad act like he didn't want to talk to me?

Finally I could see them on the other side of a guardrail. My brother looked taller than ever and was grinning lopsidedly. I couldn't wait to go around the end of the guardrail for my first embrace.

"It's just so good to be home!" I repeated, all semblance of sophisticated traveler from abroad gone.

"Look at me, I'm a mess," I said, sniffing and hunting for a hanky. "I didn't think I was going to cry again."

"How was your trip?" Mom asked.

"Long. Three nights without really sleeping," I explained. "We slept in Orly Airport instead of getting a hotel in Paris!"

Mom shook her head. "Where would you like to go for supper? We thought we would take you to a nice steak house—"

She eyed my jeans—still dirty from travel. I knew the steak house was as much for her sake as mine, since, living fifty miles from a city, she rarely had the chance to eat out.

"I'm not dressed very well," I acknowledged. All I really wanted was a hamburger.

"I've got jeans on too," my brother pointed out.

We got in the car without settling the matter. Like a baby rocked by the gentle motion of a moving car, sleep soon overcame me.

When I woke we were pulling in the long lane to our Florida farm.

"What happened to the steak house?"

"We saw how tired you were," Dad answered. "Then we decided maybe what you'd enjoy most was just some good Saturday-night hamburgers. I hope you're not disappointed."

"Disappointed? I haven't fantasized about anything else for the last five days! Thanks for letting me sleep. I know you would have enjoyed eating out, Mom."

"It's just good to have you home. It won't take long to make some hamburgers."

I wandered back to my room. It was freshly cleaned and a breeze blew in the back window. It looked so big.

Daddy brought in my suitcases. It would be good to unpack after so many days on the road, after a year of living out of two small drawers and half a closet.

"Have you decided what you'll do for a summer job?" Mom called from the kitchen.

"I think I'll rest up a week or so and then go down to Panama City [Florida] and see if I can get a job in a restaurant out on the beach."

"I wish there were a job in Blountstown for you," Mom said as I came in to the kitchen. "Maybe you could work in the shirt factory. Would you like to clean some celery for supper?"

I started breaking the stalk of celery apart. It always was my job on a Saturday night. How good it was to take part in these familiar rituals again!

"I've always wanted to spend a summer working at the beach. Hard telling what I'll be doing next summer after I graduate. I'll want to start a real job then."

"So how do things stand with you and Tobe?"

Mom finally asked the question I feared, yet I wanted to talk about him. I certainly thought about him enough, wishing I could share all the "firsts" of returning home with him.

"I still like him a lot, but I don't know. We'll just have to see what happens now. He's supposed to write me, but you know how that goes."

"He's certainly welcome to visit us anytime. You know that. St. Louis isn't that far away."

"At least he stopped asking me to marry him all the time. I think he finally realized we needed more time."

"I was praying for that."

"I know. Me too. I have peace about it," I said. But I couldn't bring myself to talk about the big hole I also felt inside without him. Was Tobe already hooked up with a new girlfriend, or perhaps an old one? Somehow it was so much easier to pour out my inner feelings to Mom on paper.

By the end of the following week, I was tired of lying around. It was time to hunt for that job. I easily found a restaurant with a Help Wanted sign out front and, with my prior experience as a waitress, was hired to begin the next day.

"We need all the help we can get on weekends," the manager said. "And your being over twenty-one is a big help, too. The younger girls aren't allowed to serve the beer and wine. You don't have any problems with that, do you?"

My heart sank. Beer? In this family-type steak house? "Huh? Problems with that? Oh, no, sir. I just didn't know you served beer and wine."

"People come to the beach on vacation; they want a good time. This ain't no bar, though," he hastened to add. "People don't ever come in just for a drink. This is a good restaurant. And we don't serve to anybody who looks lit already."

"Oh. That's fine."

"Good. See you tomorrow."

Mom and Dad were glad I had gotten a job so easily. But they were concerned about the fifty-mile commute and my coming home after 11:00 at night.

"This isn't Spain, you know," Mom said, remembering how safe we had felt there at all hours. I didn't tell her yet about needing to serve beer.

Already I was missing my daily *café con leche*. Heating up milk on the stove and mixing it with Mom's instant coffee just couldn't duplicate the señora's morning brew.

My last roll of photos from Spain were finally developed; I was delighted to be able to show Mom and Dad some photos of Tobe. The shot taken of both of us by the stranger in Plaza Cataluña would have been beautiful—looking at each other with sparkling eyes—but the photographer had moved. Blurry. Still, Mom could sense a bit of the emotion of that scene.

"He looks . . . very nice," she said picking her words. "Do you think he'll come visit us?"

"I don't know," I said truthfully. "I think I'll write him this morning and send him this."

"Well, invite him again. We'd really like to meet him," Mom repeated.

I felt good sending off the pictures that day before heading to my new job.

"This is Marie, Diane, Pat, and Bambi." The hostess showing me the ropes quickly introduced me to the other waitresses. "Here's your station. Just ask if you have any questions. We'll get real busy about 5:00 o'clock, so you eat your supper either before or after the rush."

I was glad I had spent a summer waitressing earlier in Blountstown; the routines were similar. By the third night, I felt like an old hand, especially after some new girls were hired.

"What are ya'll laughing about?" Diane nudged Pat in the lull before the rush.

"Are you ready for this?" Pat paused for effect. "Burt Reynolds wearing nuthin' but his gorgeous smile." She raised a copy of a new magazine, *Playgirl*.

"He ain't wearin' nothing at all?" squealed Marie.

"Naked as a baby's hind end."

"Oooh, let me see!"

I was embarrassed, not sure whether to crowd in for a peek or be accused of being goody-goody. As it was, the manager stepping through the kitchen door with paychecks solved my dilemma. The girls scurried back to their stations.

"You won't get your first check till next week," Marie said, stuffing hers into an old purse. "Me, I can't wait till my ex-husband gets back. I'll sock him for $140 child support he owes."

"I'm sorry," I said weakly.

"Yeah, he goes out on fishing ships for two months at a time. Two months! And it used to kill me when he went off for two weeks." Marie pushed her brown hair off her plain face. "Every two weeks when he'd come back, we'd spend all night partying. It was so great. Until he started partying with another girl. I didn't go for that kind of partying."

Marie's voice turned hard. "Had a girl friend in New Orleans, too."

Then she looked at me earnestly. "But he tried. He tried so hard to be good. He tried to stop drinking so many times."

I ached for Marie as I drove home that night. The fifty-mile drive after work was a chance to unwind, think and dream, a space in time to process all that was happening to me. Marie was so young, perhaps younger than I. Worrying about child support. I was glad she had felt free to share with me, but what could I do, except listen? What did it mean to be a Christian in this beach house restaurant? The questions had not changed. Only the locations.

On my days off I organized my Spain scrapbook and made plans for our apartment for fall. Why didn't Tobe write or call?

"Where do you go to school?" Marie asked one night.

"In Virginia. It's a small school." I didn't dare tell her or any of the girls that less than two weeks earlier I had been in Spain. They would never open up to me then. Already I was different because somehow it had leaked out that I was a college student.

"Billy's been exposed to chicken pox," Diane interrupted us. "How many days did you say till he'll pop out?"

"About ten days," Marie answered expertly. "At least he's not in school over the summer."

"Yeah, but it kind of cramps my style," Diane said, laughing. "I better not come home with hangovers when he's sick."

Here was Diane, maybe a year old than me, with a kid in school already, worrying about chicken pox and bills to pay.

"Are you going out after work tonight?" Marie asked.

"Yeah. I guess I better live it up while I can." Diane laughed.

"Hey, Melodie," Pat chimed in. "Do you want to go out with us after work?"

It felt good to be included with the gang, but I knew "out" meant a bar. Why did going to a bar here feel different than it had in Spain?

"Nah, but thanks for the invitation," I fudged. "I always have that long drive home."

"Oh, you don't have to drink anything," Pat assured me.

I was sure she had watched me the day I had to serve my first drink and saw how my hand had trembled getting the bottle of wine out of the cooler. It seemed like every time I came around, Pat found the filthiest stories to tell, sometimes making lewd insinuations about one of the new waitresses being a whore.

"Thanks just the same. I'm usually pretty tired." If I had drank wine while in Spain, I knew without question it was not the scene I wanted to be part of here. In the world, but not of it, echoed in my mind from a Sunday school class. Could they still accept me as their friend if I didn't go along with them?

Maybe I had just returned from seeing the world, but here was another world as foreign to my upbringing as Spain. Maybe I would never be called to serve abroad or in a third world country as I had often dreamed. But here were people who needed love and understanding as well as the light of Christ in their lives.

How much easier it would have been to just work at a church camp like many of my college friends, I thought. Oh, sure, you might have to deal with a few kids drinking or smoking or fooling around—but at least there were others who thought like you. Unfortunately, there didn't seem to be any one else working in this restaurant who wasn't into the party scene, even the married ones.

Finally there was a letter from Tobe. Mom put it on my bed so I'd be sure to see it when I got home from work. How she must have longed to open it. "I'm doing fine," I read, immediately aching for him in person. The letter chatted about this friend and that activity, about his mom and his family, and politely inquired about my life.

"Thanks so much for the picture of us," he concluded. "Don't worry about it being unfocused. It's beautiful—us together, smiling, sharing lives as if there were no today nor any tomorrow. Just *now* and that's all that mattered."

How poetic! I thought, but the truth of it suddenly drove a knife to my heart. It *was* beautiful but it *was* unfocused—a relationship not going anywhere. Between the lines I knew it was over in Tobe's heart, even if he never admitted it. We'd had a beautiful time but it was not the *right* time.

"Is he coming to visit us?" Mom asked the next morning, cheerful as always. She frequently hummed as she worked about her kitchen, especially on a bright sunny morning.

"I don't think so. He didn't say anything about it." Suddenly Mom's humming stopped.

I went back to my room till I thought I could eat my breakfast. Mom had been so blasted right about not wanting to see me hurt again.

"Shall we go shopping in Tallahassee on your next day off?" Mom asked when I returned to the kitchen. "Maybe we can cash in that rain check on your steak dinner."

"Sure, Mom, that would be great. I want to start getting some kitchen things for the apartment this fall. This will be my first apartment, you know."

"I can give you some things I don't use anymore."

"That would be great. Save money. I'm thinking about quitting down at Panama, anyway," I said. "Maybe try to get a job at the shirt factory here in Blountstown for the rest of the summer. I get so tired of that long drive."

"I don't blame you. Do you think they would hire you for just a month?"

"I don't know. They wouldn't have to know. I just don't like serving the drinks and stuff at the restaurant. Of course, it isn't more than one or two a week, but the girls are always talking about going out and partying."

"You don't have any business going out drinking after work."

"Don't worry. I wouldn't," I said.

Midway through the rush hour that night, Bambi asked if I could drop her off on my way home. I had served drinks for her before, as she was too young—and also too young to go bar-hopping with the older girls.

"Sure."

"Oh *could* you? My Mom had a date tonight and needed the car, but she dropped me off here, telling me to find a ride home."

"No problem. Catch you later," I said, hurrying to pick up an order. Maybe Bambi could be my friend, even though she was younger. Maybe I would dare tell her about my year in Spain and my letter from Tobe.

When it was time to get off, Bambi was waiting for me in the lounge with her sunglasses on. I didn't comment, knowing her to be a bit spacey.

"I suppose you wonder why the glasses. Well, I'm in love with Elton John and so I just wear these glasses whenever I'm not working," she explained.

"Ok-k-k-ay. . . ." I stammered.

"I wrote him a letter. I just know he's going to ask me to marry him. 'Course I don't know why I'd want to get married after everything I've seen." We got in my old, red Chevy.

"What do you mean?"

"Well, I've already had about four dads and now Mom is running around again."

"I'm sorry, Bambi," I said.

"Don't you just love Elton John?"

I kind of nodded, while Bambi rattled on. Poor girl, I thought, no wonder she fantasizes about loving a far-off singer with her own mom out running around. No, Bambi would never understand about me and Spain.

"Bye, thanks a million," Bambi called when I dropped her at her door. An empty house to come home to.

The remaining forty-five miles home flew by as I drank in the wonderfully cool night air. Northern Florida's pine tree industry scented the air with pungent smoke. The sky seemed so close out here, stars twinkling and not another headlight for miles on end. The weariness of a ten-hour shift on my feet left my body. I found myself singing hymn after good, old hymn. Suddenly I shivered and cranked up the window.

Pulling in the long drive at our farm, I could smell the earthiness of midsummer corn stalks. I parked and turned off the car. All was quiet. In the house, I knew, were Mom and Dad, perhaps curled up and warm together. What a lucky woman I was.

The Author

Melodie Miller Davis has been a writer/producer for the Media Ministries department of Mennonite Board of Missions in Harrisonburg, Va., since her graduation from Eastern Mennonite College (Harrisonburg) in 1975. In that capacity, she has written for radio programs like "Heart to Heart," "Mennonite Hour," and "Your Time."

Currently Melodie writes her own newspaper column, "Another Way" (which appears in about twenty newspapers), scripts for the *All God's People* video series, and is producer/writer of various promotional materials for numerous media. Her writing honors include three first place awards from the National Federation of Press Women. She is the author of six other books, including *On Troublesome Creek* (Herald Press), and several titles on parenting.

Since the birth of her first child in 1981, Melodie has been employed half time and spends the rest of her time parenting Michelle, Tanya, and Doreen, as well as writing books. She is married to Stuart, a Virginian.

They are members of Trinity Presbyterian Church in Harrisonburg, a house-church based congregation where Melodie is an elder.

Melodie grew up in northern Indiana. Although she has not returned to Spain since her year of college there, with Brethren Colleges Abroad, she dreams of it frequently. In her dreams, there is always some problem regarding money!